H. EDLAND

THE POCKET
ENCYCLOPAEDIA OF
ROSES
IN COLOUR

with 421 Roses reproduced in Full Colour

BLANDFORD PRESS
167 HIGH HOLBORN,
LONDON W.C.

First printing   -   May 1963
Second printing -   June 1963

Printed in Holland by The Ysel Press Ltd, Deventer

CONTENTS

ACKNOWLEDGEMENTS

The Author and the Publishers wish to make acknowledgements to the following:-

Mr. Jeremy McCabe, who photographed the great majority of the illustrations, with a sensitiveness for his subject and a patient attention to detail.

Mr. L.C. Longley of George Longley & Sons, The Nurseries Rainham, Kent, for his most generous cooperation and the extensive use made of his nurseries for the photographing of many of the roses.

Mr. G. S. Thomas for permission to photograph 15 of the Shrub Roses in the Sunningdale Nurseries, Windlesham.

A. F. Meilland, Cap D'Antibes, France, for the generous loan of more than 40 photographs.

The Conard-Pyle Company, Pa., U.S.A. for the loan of photographs.

Armstrong Nurseries, Inc., Ontario, California, U.S.A. for the loan of photographs.

Samuel McGredy & Son Ltd., Portadown, Northern Ireland, for the loan of photographs.

Alex Dickson & Sons Ltd., Newtownards, Nr. Belfast, N. Ireland for the loan of photographs.

W. Kordes' Sohne, bei Elmshorn in Holstein, Germany, for the loan of photographs.

Math. Tantau, Uetersen in Holstein, Germany for the loan of photographs.

Special acknowledgement is also made to The National Rose Society for permission to carry out photography in their grounds.

INTRODUCTION

Interest in the Rose, the Queen of Flowers, gains momentum every year, and it is largely for the purpose of meeting the demand for a means of identification that this book has been published. Never before has the ambitious project been attempted of illustrating in colour as many as 421 varieties of roses and at a price within the pockets of all. It is therefore anticipated, with some confidence, that the effort will be warmly welcomed.

To aid recognition each variety has been described and given a number coinciding with its colour illustration and also listed separately under its basic colouring; the latter to serve a dual purpose. Where the name of the variety is unknown and required to be traced from its colour, reference to the appropriate group will limit the search and make for quick reference; and/or if a variety of a particular colour is required for a special purpose, reference to the lists will aid in making a suitable selection.

Though this book is primarily intended for identification purposes, it has been thought helpful to add notes on classification, together with some brief cultural instructions.

One of the problems which had to be faced, was the order in which the illustrations fell. Should they be arranged alphabetically or grouped in colours, or by some other method?

If they were arranged alphabetically in the English language, they would be quite out of order in the French, German, Italian and other editions, because the same rose is often called by a quite different name, ('Message' in Great Britain is 'White Knight' in U.S.A.). This is an international publication, and is being printed simultaneously for six or seven other countries, so it became obvious that alphabetical order would not answer.

Then there was the idea of arrangement by colours. Here again this was quickly ruled out; if all the reds were arranged together, there would be considerable clashing and all the yellows together would seem insipid. In fact the only way in which the colour values could be brought out to full appreciation, was the arrangement of pages on a basis of colour harmony or contrast. As the most important factor in this book is the precision of the colour shades and tones, it was decided finally to arrange the pages regardless of any particular order in an endeavour to present to the reader all the colours to their fullest value. The descriptions are arranged alphabetically and there is an index at the back.

Roses are of international interest and when a new rose which has all the qualities that are desired, has been developed, it soon gains for itself a world wide reputation and establishes itself in many countries. The roses chosen for this book are those which have established themselves in popularity because of their beauty and colour or fragrance and also have stood the test of time and proved their hardiness and endurance. There are probably more than a thousand names now appearing in the catalogues, but most of those that I have chosen have proved themselves outstanding on all points and continue in popularity. Some are new to commerce but they promise well. As time goes on new stars in the rose world will rise and may-be some of the present favourites may wane. There may be some omissions but this book presents more roses than any other book ever published in comparable format and does therefore warrant the name of a Pocket Encyclopaedia. Tribute must be made to the hybridist who through his skill and knowledge, has produced the modern rose. The majority of those illustrated in these pages have been raised in France, Germany, Great Britain, Ireland, Holland, Scandinavia and America.

The outstanding feature of this book (of course) is the accuracy of the colour. Great pains have been taken all the way through the processes of photography, photo-litho and printing in order to accomplish this degree of accuracy; and to present the range of shades and the nuance of hues the illustrations have been printed in six colours. Even so, it is possible that an illustration may not have caught a favourite rose in the mood best known to the reader, for a rose can change its colour daily from the time it is in bud, until it drops its petals.

Apart from its many uses and the interest it will hold in assembling so many roses together, I hope this book will also help the reader in making a choice of roses for his garden.

H. EDLAND

St. Albans, England, February 1963

CLASSIFICATION

The Rose has long been the most popular flower and references to its beauty can be found far back in history. In those far gone days it blossomed in its natural wildness as a simple flower of five petals only; yet it is from these original species that the glorious creations of the present day have evolved—through natural cross fertilization during the early centuries and in recent years by selective breeding by hybridists.

To explain this evolution step by step is almost impossible as early records are far from complete, and these comments are restricted to providing a simple outline cf classification as it is to-day.

The extensive hybridisation which has taken place during the last century has resulted, generally speaking, in the abandonment of all effort to link current varieties to their earlier groups. This has made for simplicity; were it not for the fact that older varieties are still in cultivation, classification would present no problems, but the situation is such that it is the numerous classes of old roses which cause perplexity, especially to the uninitiated. The best way, therefore, to get to grips with the subject is to group roses into 'Old' and 'New'.

The Old Roses comprise the original species and their hybrids which, in order to distinguish them, are given the prefix 'rosa'. *Rosa* is followed by a latinised name in some cases derived botanically, in others the name of the finder, or thirdly the name of the country or area from which it originated. Three examples respectively of each of the foregoing are, *Rosa multiflora*, *Rosa canina* and *Rosa Spinosissima: Rosa banksia*, *Rosa willmottiae* and *Rosa wilsonii; Rosa chinensis; Rosa gallica* and *Rosa damascena*. It is neither necessary nor important to list the respective classifications of all the Old Roses as it follows automatically that those varieties not classified in the modern manner, as given in the following explanations, can almost certainly be accepted as being species or hybrids of species.

The New (modern) Roses which have been evolved from cross breeding the old varieties and their subsequent progeny have by now such a mixed parentage that, as stated, no attempt is made to define the relationship to their parents, and they fall mainly into two groups—the hybrid teas (H.T.) and floribundas (flori.). The hybrid tea came into being during the latter part of the last century and resulted from crossing two groups then popular, the hybrid perpetual (H.P.) and tea rose (T). The hybrid perpetuals were so named because they flowered in the autumn as well as in the summer, which distinguished them from their predecessors which were summer flowering only. The tea rose was so named because its scent was likened to that of tea. The outstanding feature of both groups was the shapeliness of their blooms, and this has been inherited by their progeny. Other classes of roses have since been merged into the hybrid teas, as for example the pernetianas (pern.) named after Pernet-Ducher who raised them, but all, with the exception of a few still propagated, have ceased to be perpetuated as separate classes of roses. In other words, hybrid tea is now used as an omnibus term to embrace all bedding varieties of roses which produce shapely full petalled blooms. A few exceptions which are semi-double, or with five petals only, which were among the first so classified can be ignored.

The floribundas are a little more involved. A few years back these roses were known as hybrid polyanthas or Poulsen roses, owing to their derivation from crossing a race of dwarf growing roses known as polyantha pompons (Poly. poms) which produce clusters of small flowers, with varieties of hybrid tea. As Poulsen of Denmark was the originator of the earliest of these his name became associated with them, and the expression 'Poulsen rose' was at one time equally as well known as hybrid polyantha. The result of the crosses were trees of the same free branching and flowering habit as the polyantha pompons but taller and with larger petalled flowers, though all were either single—i.e. five petalled—or semi-double—i.e. having two rows of petals. The polyantha pompon though still catalogued has virtually been superseded.

The hybrid polyanthas, owing to their hardiness and ease of cultivation, became very popular and hybridists experimented extensively merging into them various other strains of roses with similar habit of flowering.

Inevitably in time purists objected to the term hybrid polyantha being applied to all of this type and a compromise was reached to use the term 'floribunda' to describe the newer ones which were not a direct cross between the polyantha pompon and the hybrid tea. Latterly, however, 'floribunda' has become accepted as an omnibus term to embrace all bedding varieties of cluster flowering habit, excepting for the polyantha pompons owing to their dwarfer habit and smaller blooms, and a recent new class called polyantha compacta, which are even dwarfer growing than the polyantha pompons, and therefore suitable only for edging purposes.

Before leaving the floribundas it must be mentioned that hybridizing is still going on, and in fact on a more extensive scale than ever before, and quite naturally the hybridists are concentrating on the two main groups: the hybrid teas and floribundas. As the result of intercrossing the floribundas, which already have hybrid tea blood in them, with other hybrid teas, a few varieties have appeared on the market which, whilst still retaining in the main the cluster habit of flowering of the floribundas, also produce stems which carry fewer but fuller blooms of similar substance to the hybrid teas, even though as yet not of equal shapeliness. These varieties are presenting a problem to the authorities. In America the Nurserymen have adopted for them the term grandiflora, but in England this terms has been rejected, partly on botanical grounds and partly from the fact that the blooms are not 'grand' or 'large' (however grandiflora may be interpreted) in comparison with the hybrid tea. The term 'floribunda—hybrid tea' type is being used to describe them, though most consider it cumbersome. Very possibly in time the problem will resolve itself, as with still further improvement in the quality of the flowers such varieties will automatically be accepted as hybrid teas.

Having disposed of the two largest groups of modern roses with passing reference to other groups which have been involved in their production, all that remain are the climbers (c), ramblers (R), shrubs (s) and miniatures (min.). As these terms are self explanatory there is no necessity to dwell upon them, though perhaps it would be as well to mention that there are several types of climbing and rambling roses. Basically these fall into two groups according to the nature of their growth; the true ramblers which produce long slender pliable stems from the base each year and climbers which produce thick sturdy basal stems at infrequent intervals, the majority of their new growth coming as laterals from existing main stems. The first are listed as ramblers and the second as climbers under a variety of names and symbols according to their parentage. Examples of the latter are (C.H.T.) for the climbing forms of the hybrids tea, (CL.F.) for floribundas and so on. Some, the parentage of which is obscure, are simply known as large flowered climbers (L.F.C.). The ramblers—owing to their susceptibility to mildew—should be used to cover structures such as fences or trellis through which air flows freely, whereas the climbers are more suited for walls though they can of course be grown also on trellis or fences.

It is hoped that these comments on classification, though brief for such an involved subject, will give the reader an insight into the subject and any remaining uncertainty cleared up by the following notes on the various groups of roses to be found throughout catalogues.

MODERN ROSES

Hybrid Tea	Trees suitable for bedding purposes which in the main produce shapely blooms of good substance.
Floribunda	Likewise suitable for bedding, but primarily massed for colour effect and not for the beauty of the individual bloom.
Floribunda hybrid tea type (Grandiflora in America)	Varieties in which the characteristics of both parents, the floribunda and hybrid tea, are present, some stems producing clusters of blooms and others fewer blooms of more substance.
Polyantha Pompon (dwarf polyantha)	Trees of dwarf habit bearing clusters of small blooms. One of the parents of the hybrid polyanthas.
Hybrid Polyantha	Now an almost obsolete term, the omnibus term floribunda having replaced it to embrace the original varieties and later

introductions of similar type. Such old varieties still listed as hybrid polyanthas are strong growing, producing their single or semi-double blooms in clusters.

Polyantha compacta
A new race which, as the name implies, are compact and dwarf. Very free flowering in clusters and ideal for edging.

Miniature (Fairy Rose)
In the main very dainty dwarf growing plants, producing miniature flowers. Suitable for edging. Grown extensively in pots, but quite hardy out-of-doors.

Climber
Trees of upright climbing habit mainly summer flowering only, though a few repeat. Both types of bloom—full petalled, similar to the hybrid tea, and single or semi-double blooms of the floribunda cluster habit—are to be found in this group.

Rambler
As the name implies, of rambling habit; the varieties in this group are best suited for covering fences, pergolas, banks and trellis. Summer flowering only.

Hybrid Musk
Shrub roses which are the result of crosses between the species *Rosa moschata* and various modern roses. The blooms, which have a musk fragrance, are freely produced in early summer and intermittently for the rest of the season. In recent years there have been some notable continuous flowering additions to this Group. Excellent for hedging purposes.

Hybrid perpetual
One of the parents of the modern hybrid tea group, and now an obsolete classification.

OLD ROSES

Rosa alba
Erect shrubs, which freely produce flat blooms of good fragrance. A feature is their greyish green foliage. Summer flowering.

Rosa banksiae
A group of climbing roses which are somewhat tender and require a sheltered position. Growth strong with few thorns.

Rosa bourboniana
The 'Bourbon' rose—most develop into fine shrubs, although within the group are to be found some vigorous pillar and climbing forms. The blooms are variable in shape, though typical specimens resemble camellias. Most varieties are very fragrant.

Rosa centifolia
(The Moss Rose)

In the main the respective varieties make moderate sized shrubs 3-5 feet in height. Many have mossed flower stems.

They are descendants of the Cabbage rose, a very full petalled variety of intense fragrance.

Rosa chinensis

The Chinese or Bengal rose from which most perpetual flowering varieties have been evolved. The majority make medium bushes of 3-4 feet, but climbing forms within the group require a warm wall as they are rather tender. The stems are reddish with few thorns, and t͟ e blooms intensely fragrant.

Rosa damascena

So called because the variety was presumed to have been brought originally from Damascus. The majority in the group develop into tall slender shrubs carrying nodding loose blooms of delicious fragrance.

Rosa gallica

Also known as The 'French Rose' or 'Rose of Provins'. Shrubs of moderate height—3-5 feet—bearing flat double blooms; very fragrant.

Rose rugosa

The Japanese rose, the common variety of which is used largely as a root understock. Cultivated varieties within the group contain among them some of the best roses for hedging purposes. Many are perpetual flowering and very fragrant.

Rosa spinosissima
(The Scotch Rose)

These are dwarf growing compact plants, which being very thorny are suitable for forming thickets. Recent hybrids of the group, however, make tall shrubs carrying attractive single or semi-double flowers in early summer followed by a display of large shapely heps in the Autumn.

NOTES ON CULTIVATION

The enthusiasm for the rose is boundless, and although much has been written on its cultivation, the demand for information is so insatiable that it is unthinkable to produce a Rose Book, even one largely intended for identification purposes without going if only briefly into this matter. For ease of reference each phase of culture appears under a separate shoulder heading and automatically a start is made with:

Preparation of the soil

On this topic one can be quite dogmatic and say without fear of contradiction that nothing is more important, if one wishes to get the best out of roses, than to prepare the soil thoroughly before planting. A rose bed after being marked out requires to be dug thoroughly two spits deep over the whole area.

The usual method employed is first to take from one end of the bed a layer of the top soil roughly 15 inches wide and a spade deep and deposit it at the other end of the bed. The lower spit, thus exposed, is then forked over and thoroughly broken up and manure added. The next section of top spit is then moved over to complete the part dug, and by so doing a further 15 inches of lower spit is exposed for breaking up and manuring. This process goes on until the other end of the bed is reached, the last section of sub-soil being covered with the top spit that was placed there in readiness at the start. By working systematically in this way it ensures the fertile top spit remaining at the top, which is important. Deep cultivation has several advantages, it assists drainage, sweetens by aeration and allows the roots of the trees to penetrate further afield in search of food, and the manure improves its physical condition, and supplements the natural fertility of the soil. Farmyard or horse manure are best if obtainable, but practically anything of vegetable origin can be used—compost, leaves, leaf mould, chopped turf and even rags and wastepaper. Peat, likewise, is beneficial though for its moisture-holding capacity only, and not for nutritional value which is virtually nil. In light soil it is of more advantage to fork it into the top spit. Prepare all rose beds at least three weeks before planting to allow for consolidation.

Planting
Planting can be carried out in open weather at any time between October and April. Open up a hole in the prepared ground about 18 inches square and 12 inches deep, and place the roots of the tree in it so that the union of scion and stock is level with the surface of the surrounding soil. Spread the roots over as large an area as possible and then cover with some fine soil to which some peat and a little bone meal can be added and firm it with the hand to avoid air pockets beneath the roots; then cover with more soil and tread lightly. Replace the remainder of the soil and treat firmly. When all is finished the union of scion and stock whether of bush, shrub or climbing rose should be just below the surface. With standards, plant as shallowly as possible: the original soil mark will give the correct depth.

Standard roses are best planted at least 4 feet 6 inches apart, and bush roses 18 inches to 24 inches. Shrubs according to their vigour but not less than 4 feet, while climbing roses require a minimum of 8 feet and ramblers, 15 feet.

Transplanting
The best periods to transplant are October/November or February/March. On lifting, all foliage (if any) should immediately be stripped from the trees and while they are in hand it is as well to trim the roots, remove all twiggy growth, and as much old wood as possible. Following this, all long growths are best shortened. If the work is being carried out in February/March they can be shortened to six to nine inches, but if in October/November to nine to twelve inches to allow for possible die-back and to enable retipping in February/March. It is desirable to replant the trees with the minimum delay, and if the new beds are made ready in advance this will present no difficulty. If, however, they are to be replanted in the same bed the only course is to heel them in whilst the bed is being re-dug and manured. Whilst the trees are laying about out of the ground it is as well to cover them with sacking as a protection from cold winds.

Sometimes, owing to moving house, transplanting has to be carried out at other times than during the winter, but even so there is little risk provided care is taken to keep the trees from drying out. On lifting, and without a ball of earth around the roots as is wrongly supposed to be necessary, strip and prepare the trees as already outlined, but for the time being do not shorten the growths unless of abnormal length when they can be cut back to 15 to 18 inches. With this done, wrap the trees in wet sacking which should be kept moist during transit and until they are replanted. If there are any obstacles to replanting, it is best to heel the trees in and keep them well watered, but they should be permanently replanted as quickly as possible. If the weather is dry, syringe the stems with clean water in addition to watering the roots until the trees begin to throw new shoots, and then the stems can be cut back accordingly.

Replacements in old beds

A common mistake resulting in the failure of new trees, is the filling up of gaps in old beds without taking the precaution of renewing the soil. Where an old plant has lived for some years the soil quite naturally is exhausted, and it is essential if one wishes to give the new tree a reasonable chance of survival that this soil should be replaced. Remove a cubic foot or so of the old soil, break up the sub-soil, manure and refill with fresh top soil from another part of the garden.

Disbudding

Nearly all hybrid tea roses throw a cluster of buds. The number on the cluster varies according to the variety, some producing three, others five, while some will produce even more. If all buds are left the result will be a cluster of small poorish blooms, therefore it is necessary to disbud. To obtain the best possible blooms from hybrid teas it is advisable to remove all but the central bud and the side bud which comes a little below the main cluster, but this is purely optional, more buds can be left if so desired. With varieties of the decorative floribunda type thin out judiciously to avoid overcrowding.

Disbudding should begin as soon as the buds are formed, but

great care must be taken when so doing as the neck of the flower stem is exceedingly brittle in its early stage of growth.

Feeding

Established beds need a good mulching with organic manure annually in the Spring; alternatively a balanced fertilizer can be applied in conjunction with garden compost and peat.

In addition extra feeding in liquid form can be given from the time the buds begin to form until they flower, which is usually in about three weeks. An excellent formula is a mixture of the quick acting chemicals—Nitrate of Potash and Phosphate of Potash at the rate of half an ounce of each to three gallons of water. Apply one gallon of the liquid to the square yard, and repeat the application every five days during the formative period.

An alternative feeding, and the one more commonly used, is a liquid made from horse or farmyard manure. Some time ahead of when it will be wanted, bag up the manure and put it into a tub filled with water to soak. When the time arrives for feeding dilute the solution to a pale straw colour and apply at the rate of one gallon per tree per week.

No stimulants should be applied during a dry period without first well watering the soil and the applications are best stopped after the main flowering at the end of July so as not to induce soft lush growth late in the season. They can, however, be given in late July a final dressing of Rose Fertilizer.

Newly planted trees would also benefit from the extra feeding as above and they, as well as established trees, will also benefit if kept well watered during a dry period.

Cutting rose blooms

How long a stem may be taken with a rose bloom? The answer to this is a commonsense one, it just depends upon the vigour of the tree. An established tree bearing a quantity of wood and foliage will possibly benefit by the cutting of long stems as it is a form of summer thinning, but obviously a newly planted tree, or one that is weakly in growth, would suffer from like treatment. It should be borne in mind that there is a two way flow of sap, one rising from root action and the other through the foliage. To remove the foliage if the tree can ill spare it can only tend to debilitate, and the obvious course of action with such trees is to retain all the foliage possible. Another point of interest when cutting blooms is how to prolong their life. To put them in water right up to their necks immediately they are cut and leave them to have a good drink for some hours is the best way, and this treatment can be supplemented by adding Chrysal to the water in the receptacles used subsequently to display the blooms.

Pests

Greenfly is the chief insect enemy of the rose in the early summer, and if left unchecked can do considerable harm. There are many excellent insecticides on the market from which to choose if it is found impossible to keep the trees clean by the use of one's fingers.

Most gardeners have experienced, particularly with varieties of the Ophelia group, a malformation of the first crop of bloom and although this could be due to bad weather, another cause is Thrips (Thunderflies). These are very minute insects which get right inside the centre of the bud and destroy the organs of the flower with the result that they fail to develop in a proper manner. Owing to their habit of burrowing into the heart of the bloom these insects are difficult to combat and the only remedy is to use a deterrent such as D.D.T., when the roses are still in bud.

Disease

Mildew, Black Spot, and Rust are the three principal fungal diseases affecting roses and none, unfortunately, is easily controlled.

Mildew, which coats the flower bud and young stems with a white film, is perhaps the lesser of the three evils, but nevertheless it is very unsightly and if left to go unchecked will completely spoil the appearance of the trees and flowers. It results chiefly from sudden changes in temperature, as for example a cold night following a hot sunny day, and therein lies the trouble in controlling it. As soon as one attack is cleared more variations of temperature will start another attack. Ordinary washing soda, not exceeding an ounce to a gallon of water, is quite useful in rectifying a mild attack, but one of the proprietary fungicides is best applied if the attack spreads.

Black Spot is more serious, though it is not a killer, and the year following an attack, if the trees at the appropriate time are adequately pruned, they will grow and flower normally. Like Mildew, the disease renders the trees unsightly but a worse feature is it causes defoliation. The first symptoms start on the lower leaves and take the form of black spots (from which the disease gets its name), the spots spread and join up and gradually each leaf affected yellows and dies. Undoubtedly checks in growth caused by cold winds and drought render the foliage susceptible to attack, and while nothing can be done about cold winds, good deep cultivation of the soil in the first instance, coupled with a mulch over the beds in the summer to provide a cool root run, will tend to offset drought and to ward off attacks or lessen their severity. Spraying with a proprietary fungicide according to the makers' instructions is, however, most desirable as the disease is contagious. Picking off affected leaves is also most helpful.

Rust, which can be recognised by the reddish powder (somewhat similar to mustard) which appears on the undersides of the leaves in Summer and later turns black like soot, is a killer. Every effort, therefore, should be made to control an attack from the outset. The leaves of any tree that suddenly looks sickly should be examined immediately, and if rust is confirmed and only one tree affected the best treatment is to cut it right down to the ground at once—whatever the time of year—to safeguard other trees. This is the cheapest and most effective way of dealing with the trouble. If, however, the disease has spread before being noticed and similar drastic cutting is unpalatable, spray at once with an appropriate fungicide, taking care to wet the undersides of the leaves well. Collect and burn also, any leaves that fall to the ground.

In addition to spraying against all three diseases during the growing seasons, it is helpful during the winter to make an effort to destroy any spores that may be overwintering on the trees. In January prune the trees hard and so eliminate as much risk as possible, and then saturate the trees and surrounding soil with Copper Sulphate at the rate of 1 oz. to a gallon of water. Immediately after pruning, Copper Sulphate can again be applied, but at a weaker strength of $\frac{1}{2}$ oz. to a gallon of water, though this spray should not be used when once the trees are furnished with new foliage as it will scorch, a milder fungicide being essential during the growing season. At the beginning of May give the beds a mulch of manure or compost mixed with peat, or with the latter if that only is available. The mulch can be maintained with grass mowings.

To round off these comments on disease, it is perhaps desirable to suggest that advice first be obtained before resorting to fungicides, as quite often the enthusiastic beginner by the wrong use of chemicals does more harm than good. There should be no need to spray other than with an insecticide until the second half of the year, as earlier markings on the leaves in most instances are caused by the weather. The hot sun following rain will cause scorch and even more damage results from cold winds. The redness and curling of the foliage is due to the latter upsetting the stomata of the leaf and thus checking the creation of chlorophyl, and even though these disfigurements may be accompanied by a little mildew it is best in early summer to allow them to recover naturally than to drench with a fungicide.

Suckers

Finally, to complete this chapter on Cultivation, mention must be made of suckers. Undoubtedly everyone knows that a sucker is a wild growth, but perhaps for beginners it is as well to explain how and why roses are troubled with them. It is because the tree purchased from a grower is a budded plant in practically every instance. In other words, it is made up of two parts, top growth which is a specific cultivated variety and a root system which is of a selected strain of 'wild' rose. The purpose of marrying the cultivated rose with the wild rose by budding is to provide the former more quickly with a vigorous root system. Nevertheless there is the disadvantage that it is impossible to suppress entirely the wild root system and from time to time it sends out growths which, to distinguish them from the cultivated rose, are termed 'suckers'. If they are allowed to grow freely they will quickly outgrow the cultivated variety, therefore it is necessary to cut them away immediately they are spotted. The proper way to do it is to trace back the sucker and cut it away at its base, even though this may involve scraping the soil away from the union or a section of the roots.

Suckers which appear on the stems of standards, as they are prone to do quite freely anywhere below the point of budding, should be removed at their base and a nick cut into the stem to ensure the removal of further eyes.

There is an erroneous belief that suckers sometimes develop from the top growth, but that is impossible—they can come only from the wild rose part of the tree which is below the union. They may come from immediately below it or from the roots.

A further fallacy is that all growths are suckers which carry more than 5 leaflets to the leaf, but this is a most unreliable method of identification. A rambler rose almost always has 7 leaflets whilst bush roses, hybrid teas and floribundas, have both 5 and 7 leaflets.

The most certain way of identifying a sucker is to confirm that it comes from below the union. It is only those that are so close to the union that they appear to come from it that there should be any doubt about, but comparison of the stem and foliage of the suspect growth with that of the cultivated rose should settle the question.

PRUNING

In due course, there arises the controversial task of pruning; controversial as to when it should be done and the severity with which the trees be cut back, and for clarity it is necessary to differentiate between maidens and established trees.

PRUNING MAIDENS
(i.e. one year old trees as received from the Nursery).

Bush and Standards

With newly planted bushes and standards there is fortunately a large measure of agreement that pruning be hard the first year in order to force new growths from or near the union. The way to start is to remove completely any thin undersized stems by cutting them right down at their base. Next deal likewise with any growths that are obviously of soft wood. On maiden trees there may be neither undersized stems nor soft basal growths, but it is a possibility that has to be recognised. The tree will then consist of two or more good stout well ripened stems. Each stem in turn should be pruned to an outward pointing eye approximately five or six inches from the union, the cut being made within a quarter of an inch of the eye and sloped in the direction it is pointing. The new stems which will grow from these eyes, together with others that will break near or direct from the union, will form a good framework upon which to build in the coming years.

Shrubs

The pruning of shrubs the first year is the same in principle as that of bush or standard trees, but as they are more vigorous, the original stems can be left longer, approximately twelve to fifteen inches.

Ramblers and Climbers

Both these types of tree are best left unpruned the first year, with the exception of cutting back to sound wood in February or March any stems that have died back. Train the growths fanshape and tie them securely to their supports, using cloth as a buffer to prevent chafing or frost damage which is likely if the supports are of metal or wire.

PRUNING ESTABLISHED TREES

Bushes and Standards

In the second and subsequent years it is not essential to cut back all growths on bushes, shrubs and standards to a few inches from the union as was once considered to be desirable. Provided the main stems have not deteriorated, and generally speaking a stem retains its full vigour for approximately three years, they should be retained except for occasionally thinning them out to make way for younger stems that have come from or near the union. The new stems, however, must be well ripened and not 'water' shoots (as they are termed) which grew late in the previous season. By reason of their late appearance such shoots do not have the opportunity of ripening and, in consequence, are soft and useless and should be removed in their entirety. The approach to pruning established trees is therefore first to examine the main stems and thin out as circumstances demand and cut back the new basal growths retained on bushes, and standards to an eye five or six inches from the union. The new basal growths on shrubs can be left twelve to fifteen inches long. With this done concentrate on thinning and pruning the growths from the older wood made the previous summer. This growth will consist of sturdy laterals, and the sub-laterals which followed the first flush of bloom. These sub-laterals should all be removed and the more sturdy laterals cut back to within three or four eyes of their base. In subsequent years the new laterals from these eyes should be treated in a like manner, so that the trees are gradually built up in size.

The foregoing outline is of course the ideal and if each tree complied in every respect with this pattern of growth there would be little or nothing in pruning. Unfortunately, they do not—some varieties are constitutionally weak and subject to die-back and stems also receive damage from frost and other causes. Consequently the pruning gets a little complex and commonsense has to be used. Stems that have died back need to be cut to sound wood, likewise damaged stems to below the affected part, and if

PRUNING A TWO-YEAR OLD TREE

1 Thinning out decadent wood.
3 Reducing laterals to an even height.

2 Shortening new basal growths.
4 The pruned tree.

this leaves an unbalanced shape healthy stems will need also to be pruned in proportion. The pith of a healthy stem should be ivory white; a brown tinge indicates frost damage.

Ramblers and Climbers

As mentioned earlier, a certain amount of confusion exists in distinguishing between ramblers and climbers, and often some varieties are indiscriminately classified. In so far as pruning is concerned, however, there should be little difficulty in recognising one from the other. The true ramblers produce annually from the base a number of slender pliable stems, whereas the climbers are less prolific and the fewer stems that they send up are sturdy and unbendable. If one looks for these characteristics, even though the name of the variety may be unknown, the method of pruning is clear. The ramblers require to be drastically thinned annually, this involves cutting out from the base all or practically all the long stems produced in the previous year. The climbers with their fewer basal stems cannot be treated in a like manner, and pruning consists of occasionally thinning only. In lieu of new basal growths the climbers are apt to produce lateral growths along the length of existing stems, and as these laterals rob the top-most portions of the older stems of nourishment, from time to time it is necessary to cut away such parts as they automatically deteriorate. Sub-laterals which flowered the previous season require to be shortened to two eyes.

The time to prune

Ramblers which are Summer flowering only are best pruned in early September, in order to encourage and develop the formation of new wood.

The time to prune Climbers, Shrubs and species which break into growth early in the New Year, is December/January.

Bushes and Standard roses can be left until the end of March or beginning of April, if the blooms are required for exhibition purposes, but if this purpose is not in mind they are best pruned at the end of February.

Thinning

The removal of damaged and surplus new growths in the weeks

following is a matter of routine cultivation and not pruning in the generally accepted sense, yet, however classified, the work is of importance.

As the result of frost immediately after pruning the tips of stems often die-back and it is necessary to reprune to the next eye lower down the stems. Alternatively only the new growth may be damaged in which case the eyes invariably break afresh, but in place of one new shoot two or more will make their appearance. Obviously if all are left the result would be a cluster of spindly stems, so rub out all but one—the strongest of the new shoots. The risk of frost persists until late in May and many shoots which are several inches long before receiving damage simply go blind. Such shoots are easy to observe as they become malformed and stunted and there is only one remedy and that is to cut them right back to their base.

EXPLANATION OF ROSE TERMS

Bedding
: A somewhat ambiguous term as any variety might be used for bedding purposes, but generally it is applied to varieties of average growth which are suitable for formal beds.

Border
: A term applied to such varieties which owing to their vigour would be out of place in formal beds.

Bud
: A term applied equally to 'flower' or 'leaf' buds according to context. See also 'eye'.

Budding
: A term used in connection with propagation. It implies the operation of cutting a leaf bud (eyes) from the stem of a cultivation variety (the scion) opening the bark of an understock, inserting therein the 'bud' and binding it in.

Cut-back
: Trees which have been pruned, as distinct from trees in their first year which are known as 'maidens'.

Double Blooms
: 18-25 petals are so described.

Eye
: A term commonly used to describe a 'leaf bud'.

Full-petalled
: A term applied to rose blooms of substance.

Heeling in
: A term which indicates temporary planting until the weather improves or new beds are ready to permit permanent planting. Provided care is taken to cover the roots well with soil, trees 'heeled in' will come to no harm even if left for many weeks.

Maiden
: A 'maiden' is a tree up to twelve months old. 'Maiden growth' the first year's growth.

Reversion
: This term can refer to a cultivated variety which has been outgrown by the understock, though it is more generally applied in connection with a variety which is a throwback in colour to one of its original parents. See 'sport'.

Scion
: The cultivated variety, the leaf buds (eyes) of which are used when budding.

Seedling
: Any rose raised from seed.

Semi-double	A term applied to blooms having more than five but not more than fifteen petals.
Single flowered	A bloom having one row of five petals only.
Sport	A variety that has resulted from the freakishness of nature. An established tree of a cultivated variety will at times throw a stem carrying blooms differing in colour to the original.
Sport climbing	In a like manner to the above, a bush variety will suddenly develop climbing characteristics and thus a climbing sport is created.
Standards	Roses of the hybrid tea or floribunda type when budded at varying heights from the roots on specially selected stems are known as standards. Full standards are budded at a height of three feet six inches, half standards at approximately two feet and dwarf standards at a lesser height.
Stocks	See 'understock'.
Suckers	Growths emanating from the understock.
Summer flowering	By this is meant those varieties which flower once only in the season.
Understocks	This term is given to certain selected types of the rose species upon which cultivated varieties are budded with the object of obtaining a more vigorous root action.
Union	A term which is used to indicate the point of budding where the understock and cultivated variety have knit together.
Weeping Standards	Rambler roses budded approximately 5 feet 6 inches from the roots on specially selected stems. The top growth, which hangs down, is said to 'weep', hence the name.

ROSE SELECTIONS

The following short lists of recommended varieties, in their respective colour groups, have been compiled to aid the inexperienced when ordering new trees.

Selection I

WHITE AND WHITE FLUSHED CREAM OR PINK

Hybrid Teas
Memoriam
Message

Polly
Virgo

Floribundas
Iceberg
Yvonne Rabier

CREAM TO YELLOW

Hybrid Teas
Dorothy Peach
Ethel Sanday
Golden Melody
Grand'mere Jenny

Peace
Spek's Yellow
Sutter's Gold

Floribundas
Allgold
Chanelle
Honeymoon
Sweet Repose

APRICOT, BUFF AND ORANGE SHADES

Hybrid Teas
Bettina
Diamond Jubilee
Hawaii
Helen Traubel

Mojave

Floribundas
Alison Wheatcroft
Circus

Orangeade
Orange Sensation

LIGHT PINK

Hybrid Teas
Anne Letts
Grace de Monaco

Ophelia
Silver Lining
Stella

Floribundas
Ma Perkins
Vera Dalton

SALMON, SALMON PINK TO VERMILION

Hybrid Teas
Fritz Thiedemann
Michele Meilland
Mischief

Montezuma
Super Star

Floribundas
Anna Wheatcroft
Border Coral
Paddy McGredy
Toni Lander

DEEP PINK

Hybrid Teas
Ballet
June Park
Perfecta
Picture
Pink Favourite

Prima Ballerina
Wendy Cussons

Floribundas
Dearest
Flamenco

Jiminy Cricket
Poulsen's Pink
Queen Elizabeth
Tivoli

CARMINE TO CRIMSON RED

Hybrid Teas
Betty Uprichard
Christian Dior
Ena Harkness
Karl Herbst

Floribundas
Evelyn Fison
Firecracker
Lilli Marlene

Red Dandy
Sarabande
Soleil

DARK VELVETY CRIMSON

Hybrid Teas
Bonne Nuit
Chrysler Imperial

Crimson Glory
Josephine Bruce
Mme. Louis Laperriere

Floribundas
Dusky Maiden
Moulin Rouge

BICOLOURS, RED AND YELLOW, AND RED AND SILVER

Hybrid Teas
Charles Gregory
Gail Borden
My Choice

Piccadilly
Rose Gaujard
Sabrina

Foribundas
Daily Sketch
Masquerade
Shepherd's Delight

Selection II

VERY FRAGRANT ROSES

Hybrid Teas
Andre Le Troquer
Autumn
Charles Gregory
Chrysler Imperial
Confidence
Crimson Glory
Diamond Jubilee
Eden Rose
Elsa Arnot
Ena Harkness
Golden Dawn
Golden Melody

Grace de Monaco
Josephine Bruce
June Park
Monique
My Choice
Ophelia
Polly
President Herbert Hoover
Prima Ballerina
Red Ensign
Rubaiyat
Silver Lining
Sutter's Gold

Tally Ho
Teenager
Texas Centennial
Tiffany
Wendy Cussons
Westminster

Floribundas
Dearest
Iceberg
Lilac Charm
Orange Sensation
Sweet Repose

Shrubs
Blanc double de Coubert
Conrad F. Meyer
Penelope

Roseraie de l'Hay

Climbers & Ramblers
Albertine

Hugh Dickson
Mme. Edouard Herriot
Sweet Sultan

Selection III

REPEAT FLOWERING CLIMBERS

Aloha
Conrad F. Meyer
Danse du Feu
Elegance
Gloire de Dijon

Guinee
High Noon
Hugh Dickson
Leverkusen
Maigold

Meg
New Dawn
Soldier Boy
Zephirine Drouhin

Selection IV

HARDY CLIMBERS FOR NORTH AND EAST WALLS

Conrad F. Meyer
Danse du Feu
Hugh Dickson

Leverkusen
Maigold
New Dawn

Soldier Boy

Selection V

VARIETIES WHICH WILL PRODUCE LARGE SPECIMEN BLOOMS FOR EXHIBITION PURPOSES

Anne Letts
Ardelle
Ballet
Bayadere
Burnaby
Christian Dior
Chrysler Imperial
Claude
Crimson Glory
Diamond Jubilee
Dorothy Anderson
Dorothy Peach
Eden Rose
Elsa Arnot
Emily
Ena Harkness
Ethel Sanday
Fritz Thiedemann
Gail Borden

Golden Dawn
Golden Masterpiece
Golden Melody
Gordon Eddie
Grace de Monaco
Grand'mere Jenny
Hawaii
Isabel de Ortiz
June Park
Karl Herbst
Lucy Cramphorn
Margaret
McGredy's Ivory
Memoriam
Montezuma
Mrs. Henry Bowles
My Choice
Opera

Paris Match
Perfecta
Peace
Phyllis Gold
Pink Favourite
Pink Peace
Red Ensign
Rose Gaujard
Rubaiyat
Sabrina
Silver Lining
Stella
Sutter's Gold
Suspense
Symphonie
Tiffany
Tzigane
Wendy Cussons
Westminster

Selection VI

RECURRENT FLOWERING VARIETIES SUITABLE FOR SHRUBS
OR HEDGES 4 FT AND OVER. PLANT 3 FT APART.

Buisman's Triumph
Buff Beauty
Friedrich Heyer

Gay Vista
Kathleen Ferrier
Nymphenberg
Penelope

Prosperity
Queen Elizabeth
Sarah Van Fleet

Selection VII

RECURRENT FLOWERING VARIETIES SUITABLE FOR HEDGES UP
TO 4 FT PLANT 2 FT APART.

Ama
Enterprise
First Choice
Florence Mary Morse
Frensham

Iceberg
Lavender Lassie
Magenta
Masquerade
Orange Triumph

Salmon Perfection
Shepherd's Delight
Tivoli
Yvonne Rabier

THE ILLUSTRATED PAGES

The illustrations are not arranged in any special order but the Descriptions of Varieties commencing on page 129 are in alphabetical order. The synonymous names are also listed. A full Index is at the back.

1	Golden Dawn	2	August Seebauer
3	Red Ensign	4	Lucy Cramphorn
5	Moonbeam	6	Duet

7	Fred Streeter	8	Bayadere
9	Chantre	10	Mme. L. Dieudonne
11	Florida von Scharbeutz	12	Radar

13	Chrysler Imperial	14	Golden Melody (Irene Churruca)
15	Gold Crown (Goldkrone)	16	Perfecta (Kordes Perfecta)
17	Ballet	18	Dame de Coeur

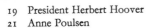

19 President Herbert Hoover   20 Karl Herbst
21 Anne Poulsen   22 Montezuma

23 Invitation
25 Royal Highness
24 Fascinating
26 War Dance

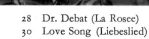

27   Tapestry
29   Pink Favourite

28   Dr. Debat (La Rosee)
30   Love Song (Liebeslied)

31 Michele Meilland
33 Grey Pearl (The Mouse)

32 Rumba
34 Salmon Perfection

35   Aztec
37   Columbus Queen

36   El Capitan
38   Taffeta

39 Stadt Rosenheim
41 Faust (Dr. Faust)
40 Bajazzo
42 Iceberg (Schneewittchen)

43   Ama
45   Elysium

44   Honeymoon
46   Prima Ballerina

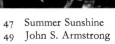

47 Summer Sunshine   48 Garden Party
49 John S. Armstrong   50 Mirandy

51 Crimson Glory
53 First Love

52 Copper Delight
54 Beauté

55　Allgold
57　Garten Zauber

56　Alison Wheatcroft
58　Rodeo

59   Claude   60   Angela

61   Buccaneer   62   Coy Colleen

63 Diamond Jubilee   64 Dairy Maid
65 Dearest   66 Carrousel

67 Mme. Henri Guillot
69 My Lady

68 Mrs. Henry Bowles
70 Masquerade

71 Marella
73 Eden Rose

72 Rendez-vous (Day of Triumph)
74 Baccara

75 Burnaby

76 Highlight

77 Silver Lining

78 Elinor le Grice

79 Texas Centennial   80 Orange Sensation
81 Flamenco   82 Fantasia

83 Belle Blonde
85 Charlotte Armstrong
87 High Society

84 Betty Uprichard
86 Brilliant (Detroiter. Schlosser's Brilli
88 Hawaii

52

89 Countess of Dalkeith
91 Comtesse Vandal
93 Burning Love (Amour Ardent. Brennende Liebe)
90 Cleopatra (Kleopatra)
92 Circus
94 Charles Gregory

53

95 Dreamland (Traumland)   96 Fanfare
97 Starfire   98 Golden Jewel

99 Helen Traubel
101 Fandango

100 Goldilocks
102 Enterprise

103 Phyllis Gold
105 Picture

104 Ophelia
106 Mojave

107 Gentle
109 Fred Howard

108 Gay Lady
110 Henry Morse

111 Korona
113 Red Favourite (Holländerin.
Schweizer Gruss)
115 Poulsen's Pink

112 Chic
114 Red Wonder
116 Paprika

58

117 Farandole
119 Piccadilly
121 Fire King

118 Florence Mary Morse
120 Happiness (Rouge Meilland)
122 Yellowhammer

123   Kathleen Ferrier
125   Prestige

124   Orange Triumph
126   Poulsen's Bedder

127 Rose Gaujard
129 Profusion
128 Red Dandy
130 Queen Elizabeth

131 Rimosa

132 Rosemary Gandy

133 Ardelle

134 McGredy's Sunset

135   Golden Masterpiece   136   Spartan
137   Scarlet Marvel   138   June Bride

151 Shot Silk
153 June Opie

152 Pepe
154 Sherry

155 Sarabande
156 Zambra

157 McGredy's Yellow   158 Cecile Brunner
159 Dr. A. J. Verhage   160 The People

           161 Fashion

162 Tony Lander
164 Chanelle

163 Daily Sketch
165 Dorothy Wheatcroft

166 Cyclamen   167 Paris-Match
168 Radway Sunrise   169 Woburn Abbey

174 Lady Maisie Robinson 175 Lilac Charm
176 Sir Winston Churchill 177 Park Direktor Riggers

178 Concerto
179 Polka

180 Fanny Blankers-Koen
182 Peach Glow

181 Flaming Sunset
183 Party Dress

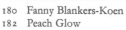

74

184   Peace (Gioia. Gloria Dei. Mme.
       A. Meilland)
186   Tzigane

185   Suspense
187   Chicago Peace

188 Display

189 Gold Cup

190 Symphonie

191 Dusky Maiden

192 New Yorker
194 Miss France
193 McGredy's Ivory
195 Lavender Lassie

196 La Jolla
198 Jiminy Cricket

197 Lal
199 Karen Poulsen

200   Marjorie le Grice
202   Ma Perkins

201   Miracle
203   Feurio

204 Jane Lazenby   205 Isabel de Ortiz
206 Paddy McGredy   207 Lavender Girl

208   Lady Belper
210   Independence (Kordes Sonder-
      meldung. Reina Elisenda)

209   June Park
211   Ena Harkness

212 Vilia
214 Moulin Rouge
213 Virgo
215 Dany Robin

216 Dickson's Flame   217 Shepherd's Delight
218 Spek's Yellow   219 Sweet Repose
      (Golden Sceptre)   (The Optimist)   83

220 Mischief
222 Salmon Marvel

221 Gertrude Gregory
223 Wendy Cussons

224　Gloria Mundi　　　225　High Noon
226　Heidelberg　　　227　Bacchus

228   Elsa Arnot   229   Border Coral
230   Summer Song   231   Bonne Nuit

232   United Nations   233   Vogue
234   Yvonne Rabier   235   Blossom Time

236 Christopher Stone   237 Salute
238 Hassan   239 Ruth Leuwerik

240 Message (White Knight)
241 Pink Peace

242   Monique   243   Lydia
244   Mahagona   245   Firecracker

246 Bonnie Maid
248 Mme. Louis Laperrière

247 Hebe
249 Lady Sylvia

250 Isobel Harkness   251 Thais (Lady Elgin)
252 La Jolie   253 Donald Prior

260 Autumn
262 Condesa de Sastago

261 Doreen
263 Ascot

264 Vive la France
266 Poulsen's Supreme

265 Lilac Time
267 My Fair Lady

268	Ethel Sanday	269	Bingo
270	Dorothy Anderson	271	Dorothy Peach
272	Emily	273	Gustav Frahm

280 Bettina
281 Grace de Monaco
282 Anne Letts
283 Alain
98 284 André le Troquer
285 Anna Wheatcroft

286	Tally Ho	287	Stella
288	Rubaiyat	289	Serenade
290	Super Star (Tropicana)	291	Chanteclerc

292 Sutters Gold
294 Fervid
296 Diablotin

293 Buff Beauty
295 Soleil
297 Ohlala

298 Allotria
300 Mme. René Coty
302 Sun Dance

299 Orangeade
301 Magenta
303 Friedrich Heyer

326 Pink Parfait   327 Nocturne
328 Suzon Lotthe   329 Forty-Niner

330　Lubeck
332　Lunelle

331　Sterling Silver
333　Cynthia Brooke

SHRUB ROSES

340 Nevada

341 Frühlingsgold   342 Frühlingsanfang
343 Frühlingsduft   344 Frühlingsmorgen

351 Frühlingsgold

352 Spinosissima - Double Yellow   353 Spinosissima Lutea Maxima

113

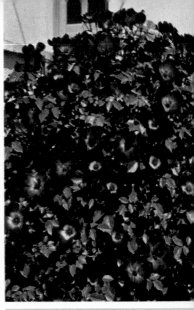

360 Elmshorn
362 St. Pauli

361 Cocktail
363 Golden Showers

370 Kassel
372 Dortmund
371 Berlin
373 F. J. Grootendorst

CLIMBERS and RAMBLERS

379 Albertine

380 Raymond Chenault   381 Köln am Rhein

382   Danse des Sylphes   384   Mermaid
383   The New Dawn   386   Sweet Sultan
385   Paul's Lemon Pillar

387 Guinee   388 Aloha

       389 Clair Matin

390 Emily Gray
392 Clg. Mme. Caroline Testout

391 Elegance
393 American Pillar

394   Zepherine Drouhin   395   Danse du Feu (Spectacular)

396   Leverkussen   397   Grandmère Jenny

398   Clg. Grandmère Jenny

399 Crimson Conquest   400 Crimson Shower
401 Alberic Barbier   402 Excelsa
124   403 Dr. W. van Fleet   404 Allen Chandler

405 Mme. Gregoire Staechelin
      (Spanish Beauty)
407 Clg. Mme. Edouard Herriot

406 Meg
408 Lady Gay

415   Baby Masquerade
416   Cameo

417 Colibri

418 Dwarf King   419 Perle de   420 Baby Gold Star   421 Presumida
128   (Zwergkönig)   Montserrat   (Estrelita de Oro)   (Peter Pan)

DESCRIPTIONS OF VARIETIES

The descriptions which follow are listed in alphabetical order.

The name of the variety is followed by its plate number, classification, then the name of its raiser together with the date the variety was first put into commerce, and finally a general description to assist identification. In respect of vigour of growth, it will be realized that the respective heights given are purely approximate as trees vary in performance from one garden to another, their vigour depending upon a number of factors—soil, cultivation and environment among others. It is thought worthwhile, however, to give a general indication, as such information is relative and useful when the planning of beds is under consideration.

In respect of fragrance, over which there is much difference of opinion, (often it is a matter of individual appreciation), to avoid controversy it is indicated by the expressions fragrant, slightly fragrant or very fragrant.

Alain. (283) FLORI. MEILLAND 1946. (Guinee × Wilhelm) × Orange Triumph.
Ovoid bud developing into medium sized semi-double flower with slight fragrance. Bright scarlet crimson. Produced in clusters. Foliage dark and glossy. Growth upright, approx. 2½ ft.

Alberic Barbier. (401) R. BARBIER 1900. R. wichuraiana × Shirley Hibberd.
Small yellow bud, flower flat creamy white with yellow centre, fragrant, full. Produced in clusters. Foliage dark and glossy, small. A rampant grower suitable for fences, trellis, pergolas. Early June flowering.   15 ft.

Albertine. (379) R. BARBIER 1921. R. wichuraiana × Mrs. Arthur Robert Waddell.
Buds coppery opening to bright pink. Flowers medium size produced in large trusses. Fragrant. Summer flowering. Light green foliage. Growth vigorous. 15 ft.

Allen Chandler. (404) CL. H.T. CHANDLER 1923. Hugh Dickson × unnamed variety.
Long pointed bud; flower brilliant crimson, large, single to semi-double. Produced several together. Slight fragrance. A suitable variety for growing on walls. Summer flowering only.

Allgold. (55) FLORI. LE GRICE 1958. Goldilocks × Ellionor Le Grice.
Bright butter-cup yellow slightly fragrant flowers. Large and semi-double, 15-22 petals produced singly or several together. Bushy and robust of even growth up to 2 ft. 6 in. Very free flowering and undoubtedly the best yellow floribunda yet produced.

Alison Wheatcroft. (56) FLORI. WHEATCROFT 1959. Sport of Circus.
Flowers deep apricot edged and flushed with crimson, large and semi-double 25 petals. Fragrant. A more colourful and robust variety than the parent. Tall upright growth up to 3 ft.

Allotria. (298) FLORI. TANTUS 1958. Red Favourite × Kathe Duvigneau.
Medium sized, semi-double blooms 14 petals, orange scarlet in colour. Slight fragrance Free flowering and moderately vigorous, up to 2 ft. 6 in.

Aloha. (388) L.F.C. BOERNER 1949. Mercedes Gallart × New Dawn.
Bud ovoid; large double, cupped rose-pink flowers with deeper reverse. Fragrant. Dark leathery foliage. An excellent pillar rose, and repeat flowering. 10 ft.

Ama. (43) FLORI. KORDES 1955. Obergartner Wiebicke × Independence.
Deep orange-scarlet very large, high centred double flowers. Produced in large clusters. Dark, glossy leathery foliage. Very free flowering, and vigorous up to 3 ft. 6 ins.

American Pillar. (393) R. VAN FLEET 1902. (R. wichuraiana × R. setigera) × red Hybrid Perpetual.
Blooms medium size, single, produced in large trusses. Carmine pink with white eye, golden stamens; non recurrent. Foliage leathery and glossy. Vigorous up to 20 ft.

Amour Ardent (93) See Burning Love

André le Troquer. (284) H.T. MALLERIN 1946.
Large, double, 30 petals, cupped flowers of orange to apricot colouring. Very fragrant. Dark foliage. A very attractive variety of moderate height up to 2 ft. 6 in.

Angela. (60) FLORI. KORDES 1957. Masquerade × Spek's Yellow.
Flowers golden yellow shaded crimson, double, 28 petals medium sized. Slight fragrance. Produced in large trusses. Dark glossy foliage. A tall upright variety which flowers freely. Approx. 3 ft 6 in.

Anna Wheatcroft. (285) FLORI. TANTAU 1959.
Shapely bud opening flat to 4 in. semi-double. Slight fragrance. Light vermilion. Medium green foliage. Growth robust and bushy. 2 ft. 6 in.

Anne Letts. (282) H.T. LETTS 1954. Peace × Charles Gregory.
Flowers pointed, large and double, 28 petals two tone pink with silvery reverse. Slight fragrance. Glossy foliage. Exceptionally free flowering, though it dislikes excessive wet. 2 ft. 6 ins.

Anne Poulsen. (21) FLORI. POULSEN 1935. Ingar Olsson × a red Hybrid Tea.
Large semi-double flowers of bright crimson-red colouring which darkens with age. Fragrant. Produced in clusters. Very vigorous reaching a height of 4 ft. and more—best suited for a border. Susceptible to Black Spot.

Ardelle. (133) H.T. EDDIE 1957. Mrs. Charles Lamplough × Peace.
Creamy white flowers, high centred large and double. 72 petals. Fragrant.

Glossy foliage. A tall upright grower up to 3 ft. Blooms inclined to ball in excessive wet.

Ascot. (263) FLORI. DICKSON 1962. Brownie × seedling.
Blooms large, semi-double, opening to 4 in. Salmon coral. Slight fragrance. Produced in trusses. Foliage large, mid green. Growth robust, dwarf and bushy. 18 in. to 2 ft.

August Seebauer. (2) FLORI. KORDES 1944. Break o'Day × Else Poulsen.
Bud long pointed, light rose opening to deep pink. Flowers large, double and high-centred. Fragrant. Produced in clusters. Glossy foliage. Average height 2 ft.

Autumn. (260) H.T. CODDINGTON 1928. Sensation × Souv. de Claudius Pernet.
Cupped full flowers of burnt-orange colouring streaked with red. Very fragrant. Free flowering. Dark glossy foliage. Growth tall and upright. 3 ft.

Aztec. (35) H.T. ARMSTRONG NURSERIES 1958. Charlotte Armstrong × unnamed seedling.
Buds long pointed and plum coloured; blooms large and full 22-28 petals opening to salmon-pink. Fragrant. Free flowering. Dark green leathery foliage. Very vigorous 3 ft. 6 in. Similar to the variety Montezuma but general performance not so good.

Baby Gold Star. (420) MIN. DOT. 1940. Eduardo Toda × R. rouletti.
Blooms small, semi-double 12-15 petals, golden yellow. Slight fragrance. Small foliage. Growth vigorous for its class. 18 in.
Syn. Estrellita de Oro.

Baby Masquerade. (415) MIN. TAN-

TAU 1956. Tom Thumb × Masquerade.
Very small (1 in.) flowers, double 20-25 petals and open, colour deep yellow to rose-red. Slight fruity fragrance. Leathery foliage. One of the most attractive of the miniatures, growing to a height of approx. 15 in.

Baccara. (74) H.T. MEILLAND 1956. Happiness × Independence.
Globular shaped bud developing into medium sized double 72-82 petals cupped flowers opening flat. Bright geranium-red. Dark leathery foliage. An upright grower up to approx. 3 ft. The blooms last well when cut and for this reason it is grown extensively under glass for the cut flower trade.

Bacchus. (227) H.T. A. DICKSON 1951. Flowers long, full 25 petals and shapely, carmine pink. Fragrant. Vigorous approx. 2 ft. 6 in.

Bajazzo. (40) H.T. KORDES 1962. Blooms very large, full, with high pointed centre. Purplish red inside of petals with white reverse. Fragrant. Growth vigorous and upright. 3 ft.

Ballet. (17) H.T. KORDES 1958. Florex × Karl Herbst.
Large, double 52 petals deep pink flowers. Only very slight fragrance. Attractive grey-green foliage. An excellent variety which produces a large quantity of shapely blooms throughout the season. If only it had a pronounced scent! Vigorous and upright, 2 ft. 6 in.

Bayadere. (8) H.T. MALLERIN 1954. R.M.S. Queen Mary × unnamed seedling.
Flowers very large, double 52 petals and high centred. Multi-coloured—salmon-pink to canary-yellow tinted pink. Slight fragrance. Dark bronzy foliage. Vigorous 2 ft. 6 in.

Beauté. (54) H.T. MALLERIN 1953. Mme. Joseph Perraud × Unnamed seedling.
Well formed double 28 petals, flowers of a light orange colour. Fragrant. An attractive variety of unusual colouring. Moderately vigorous. 2 ft. 4 inches.

Belle Blonde. (83) H.T. MEILLAND 1955. Peace × Lorraine.
Bright yellow well formed flowers, centre deeper yellow. Fragrant. A good bedding variety of moderate growth up to 2 ft.

Berlin. (371) SHRUB. KORDES 1949. Eva × Peace.
Large single orange-scarlet flowers with golden centre. Fragrant. Produced in large clusters. Dark leathery foliage. A vigorous free flowering bushy shrub reaching 6 ft. in height.

Bettina. (280) H.T. MEILLAND 1953. Peace × (Mme. Joseph Perraud × Demain)
Well formed large double flowers 37 petals salmon-orange heavily veined. Fragrant. Dark bronzy glossy foliage. Vigorous. 2 ft. 6 in.

Betty Uprichard. (84) H.T. A. DICKSON 1922.
Blooms medium six, 20 petals produced freely. Distinctive colouring—salmon pink flushed copper with carmine reverse. Fragrant. Light green foliage. Very vigorous up to 3 ft. 6 in.

Bingo. (269) H.T. ROBICHON 1955. (Hadley seedling × Ami Quinard) × Crimson Glory.
Blooms cardinal red, large, full, 45-60 petals, very fragrant. Free flowering. Growth upright and vigorous. 2 ft. 6 in.

Blanc Double de Coubert. (375)

SHRUB. COCHET-COCHET 1892. R. rugosa × Sombreuil.
Large full flat white blooms. Very fragrant. Handsome rugosa foliage. Growth vigorous and bushy up to 6 ft.

Blossom Time. (235) SEMI-CLIMBER. O'NEAL 1951. New Dawn × unnamed Hybrid Tea.
Blooms large and full, 35-40 petals, light pink with deeper reverse, freely produced in small clusters. Very fragrant. A pillar rose or shrub up to 6 ft.

Bonne Nuit. (231) H.T. COMBE 1956.
Slender buds opening to well formed medium sized flowers, full. Blackish velvety crimson. Fragrant. Lightish green foliage medium size. Growth upright, slender tree. 3 ft.

Bonnie Maid. (246) FLORI. LE GRICE 1951.
Attractive silvery pink flowers, reverse deep pink; large and semi-double 17 petals. Produced in medium sized clusters. Foliage dark and leathery. Vigorous up to 3 ft.

Border Coral. (229) FLORI. DE RUITER 1957. Signal Red × Fashion.
Medium sized (2½ in.). Semi-double, coral-salmon tinted yellow at base. Produced in clusters. Fragrant. Glossy dark green foliage. Growth robust and spreading. 2 ft.

Brennende Liebe (93) See Burning Love.

Brilliant. (86) H.T. KORDES 1952. Poinsettia × Crimson Glory. Large, double 20-25 petals, high centred flowers. Carmine overcast spectrum red. Slight fragrance. A variety which freely produces blooms of excellent quality, but a moderate grower. Up to

2 ft. Syn. Schlosser's Brilliant. Syn. Detroiter.

Buccaneer. (61) H.T. SWIM 1952. Golden Rapture × (Max Krause × Capt. Thomas).
Medium sized cupped butter-cup yellow flowers of 30 petals. Fragrant. Dark leathery foliage. A very tall growing variety best suited for a border 4 ft.

Buff Beauty. (293) SHRUB. Raiser and date unrecorded.
A moderately vigorous shrub of 4-5 ft. with arching branches. Blooms large, apricot yellow. Sweetly scented.

Buisman's Triumph. (140) SHRUB. Buisman 1952. Kathe Duvigneau × Tantau's Triumph.
Deep pink semi-double blooms produced in clusters, repeat flowering. Fragrant. Deep green foliage. Vigorous and will make a good bush up to about 4 ft.

Burnaby. (75) H.T. EDDIE 1954. Phyllis Gold × President H. Hoover.
Flowers large and very full 56 petals, high centred; canary-yellow with creamy outer petals. Slight fragrance. Glossy dark foliage. Vigorous. 2 ft. 6 in.

Burning Love. (93) FLORI. H.T. type. TANTAU 1956. Fanal × Crimson Glory.
Flowers scarlet, large and double 22 petals. Fragrant. Small trusses freely produced. Glossy dark foliage. Vigorous and bushy. 2 ft. 6 in. Syn. Amour Ardent. Syn. Brennende Liebe.

Cameo. (416) POLY.POM. DE RUITER 1932. Sport of Orleans Rose.
Flowers salmon-pink turning to soft orange-pink with age very small, semi-double, cupped. Produced in clusters.

Profuse bloom. Height approx. 18 in.

Cantab. (345) SHRUB. HURST 1927. R. nutkana × Red Letter Day.
Lilac pink blooms with attractive cream stamens. Single. Fragrant. It flowers at midsummer followed later with big dark red oval heps. Foliage dark, 7-9 leaflets. Height 8 ft.

Carminetta. (349) SHRUB. CENTRAL EXPERIMENTAL. FARM 1923. T. rubrifolia. × R. rugosa.
Pale pink single blooms produced in clusters. Slightly fragrant. Summer flowering followed by large clusters of heps. Foliage bronzy. Vigorous and bushy up to 6 ft.

Carrousel. (66) FLORI H.T. type. DUEHRSEN 1950. Unnamed seedling × Margy.
Dark red flowers, medium sized semi-double 20 petals. Fragrant. Dark glossy leathery foliage. Upright bushy growth. 2 ft. 6 in.

Cecile Brunner. (158) PLY. PERNET-DUCHER 1881. Polyantha × Mme. de Tartas.
Blooms miniature and perfectly formed. Bright pink, yellow base. Fragrant. Foliage sparse, dark green. Growths long and slender. 3 ft.

Celebration. (170) FLORI. DICKSON 1961. Dickson's Flame × Circus.
Blooms medium size, full and shapely produced in large clusters. Light salmon red with ivory reverse, flushed peach. Slight fragrance. Medium green foliage. Growth vigorous and bushy. 2 ft. 6 in.

Champs-Elysées. (323) H.T. MEILLAND 1957. Monique × Happiness.
Rich crimson-red flowers, large double

35 petals and cupped. Slight fragrance, free flowering. Vigorous and upright. 2 ft. 6 in. to 3 ft.

Chanelle. (164) FLORI. MCGREDY 1958. Ma Perkins × (Mrs. Wm. Sprott × Fashion).
Cream shading to yellow at base. Blooms shapely in bud, semi-double opening flat 2½ in. Produced in clusters. Fragrant. Growth vigorous. 2 ft. 6 in.

Chanteclerc. (291) FLORI. CAUJARD 1956. Peace × unnamed seedling.
Bright red blooms, full and large freely produced. Light green foliage. Vigorous and bushy. 2 ft. 6 in.

Chantre. (9) H.T. KORDES 1958. (Luis Brinas × Spek's Yellow) × Antheor.
Blooms large, high centred, full 20-25 petals, slightly fragrant. Orange suffused golden yellow. Very vigorous and upright. 3 ft.

Charles Gregory. (94) H.T. VERSCHUREN 1947.
Medium sized shapely blooms of 18-25 petals, freely produced. Colour vermilion shaded gold becoming lighter with age. Fragrant. Dark glossy foliage. Moderately vigorous. 2 ft. 6 in. Very attractive in early stage.

Charlotte Armstrong. (85) H.T. LAMMERTS 1940. Soeur Thérèse × Crimson Glory.
Blood red long pointed buds which produce large, double blooms 35 petals, spectrum-red to cerise, very attractive in early stage. Fragrant. Dark leathery foliage. Moderately vigorous, subject to die-back, Height approx. 2 ft.

Chic. (112) FLORI. BOERNER 1953. Pinnochio seedling × Fashion.

Blooms medium size, very full 65-70 petals, cupped and fragrant. Produced in clusters. Geranium pink. Growth vigorous and branching. 2 ft.

Chicago Peace. (187) H.T. JOHNSTON 1962. Sport of Peace.
Blooms large, full and high-centred pink, reverse gold. Slight fragrance. Growth vigorous. 4 ft.

China Town. (376) SHRUB. POULSEN 1963.
Blooms full and flat, 4½ in. across, golden yellow occasionally flushed pink, freely produced in large trusses. Repeat flowering. Fragrant. Large mid green foliage. Growth vigorous and bushy. 4-5 ft.

Christian Dior. (316) H.T. MEILLAND 1961. (Sondermeldung × Happiness) × (Peace × Happiness).
Blooms large and full, velvety scarlet inside of petals, dull scarlet on reverse, produced on strong stems. Slight fragrance. Growth vigorous and upright. 2 ft. 6 in.

Christopher Stone. (236) H.T. ROBINSON 1935. Etoile de Hollande × Hortulanus Budde.
Scarlet, overlaid crimson flowers; large, full and open. Pleasant damask fragrance. Bright green foliage. Vigorous. 2 ft. 6 in.

Chrysler Imperial. (13) H.T. LAMMERTS 1952. Charlotte Armstrong × Mirandy.
Large, full 40-50 petals, high centred flowers, crimson-red with darker shadings inclined to blue with age. Very fragrant. Large dark matt foliage. Growth vigorous and upright. 3 ft.

Circus. (92) FLORI. SWIM 1956. Fandango × Pinocchio.

Medium sized double 45-58 petals, high-centred flowers. Attractive colouring—yellow marked pink, salmon and scarlet. Fragrant. Produced in large clusters. Leathery matt foliage. Growth vigorous and bushy. 2 ft.

Clair Matin. (389) SEMI-CLIMBER. MEILLAND 1962. Fashion × (Sondermeldung × Orange Triumph) × Phyllis Bide.
Blooms medium size, cupped, semi-double, slightly fragrant, produced in clusters. Pink. Moderately vigorous, best suited for pillar.

Claude. (59) H.T. MALERIN 1950.
Very large full 35 petals; bright orient red colouring. Fragrant. Dark glossy foliage. Vigorous upright. 3 ft. Susceptible to Black Spot.

Cleopatra. (90) H.T. KORDES 1955.
(Walter Bentley × Condesa de Sastago) × Spek's Yellow.
Well formed scarlet flowers with old gold reverse, medium-sized and full 45 petals. Fragrant. Dark glossy foliage. An attractive bi-colour but moderate grower up to 18 inches. Syn. Kleopatra.

Cocktail. (361) SHRUB. MEILLAND 1957. (Independence × Orange Triumph) × Phyllis Bide.
Flowers small and single, colour geranium red overshaded crimson with primrose-yellow eye. Produced in large clusters. Glossy leathery foliage. A free flowering shrub up to 5 ft.

Colibri. (417) MIN. MEILLAND 1960.
Small apricot shaded orange blooms produced several together. Growth dwarf up to 15 in.

Columbus Queen. (37) H.T. ARMSTRONG 1963. La Jolla × unnamed seedling.

Blooms medium size, full and shapely. Soft pink inner petals, reverse magenta pink. Slight fragrance. Rich large glossy green foliage. Growth vigorous 3 ft. to 4 ft. producing blooms freely on good stout stems.

Comtesse Vandal. (91) H.T. LEENDERS 1932. (Ophelia × Mrs. Aaron Ward) × Souv. de Claudius Pernet.
Orange-copper bud developing into salmon-pink flower with coppery-pink reverse; large, double 30 petals and high centred. Fragrant. Leathery foliage. An attractive variety which produces high quality blooms, but inclined to mildew.

Concerto. (178) FLORI. MEILLAND 1953. (Alain × Floradora).
Medium sized semi-double flowers 12-17 petals, spectrum-red in colour. Slight fragrance. Produced freely in trusses. Dark green foliage. Growth bushy up to 2 ft.

Condesa de Sastago. (262) H.T. DOT. 1932. (Souv. de Claudius Pernet × Marechal Foch) × Margaret McGredy.
Large full but flat flowers, produced in small clusters. Colour oriental red with yellow reverse. Fragrant. Glossy dark foliage. Growth vigorous and bushy. 2 ft. 6 in. to 3 ft.

Confidence. (317) H.T. MEILLAND 1953. Peace × Michele Meilland.
Large, full 28-38 petals, high centred flowers of pearly light pink suffused with yellow. Fragrant. Dark leathery foliage. Vigorous and bushy. 2 ft.

Conrad F. Meyer. (354) SEMI-CLIMBER. MULLER 1899. Rosa rugosa hybrid × Gloire de Dijon.
Blooms large, cupped and full, silvery pink produced in clusters. Very fragrant. Handsome foliage, leathery and

large. Very thorny. Growth vigorous 8-10 ft. A good pillar or shrub rose.

Copper Delight. (52) FLORI. LE GRICE 1956. Goldilocks × Ellinor Le Grice. Flowers coppery orange, large and semi-double 14 petals, freely produced in clusters. Fragrant. Olive-green foliage. Vigorous and spreading. 2 ft.

Countess of Dalkeith. (89) FLORI. DOBBIE 1957.
Sport of Fashion. Flowers large, full and flat, freely produced in clusters. Vermilion flushed orange flowers. Very fragrant. Bushy growth of average height 2 ft. An attractive variety but similar to parent, subject to Black Spot.

Coy Colleen. (62) H.T. MCGREEDY 1953. (Modesty × Portadown Glory) × Phyllis Gold.
Rosy white pointed buds developing into well formed milky white flowers of medium size, full. Slight fragrance. Moderately vigorous. 2 ft.

Crimson Conquest. (399) R. CHAPLIN BROS. 1931. Sport of Red-Letter Day. Velvety scarlet-crimson flowers, small and semi-double. Light green foliage. A vigorous rampant growing variety.

Crimson Glory. (51) H.T. KORDES 1935. Catherine Kordes seedling × W. E. Chaplin.
Deep velvety crimson flowers with purple shadings; large and full; cupped. Very fragrant. Leathery foliage. Growth vigorous, flowers produced on short branching stems. Height 2 ft. to 2 ft. 6 in. An excellent standard.

Crimson Shower. (400) R. NORMAN 1951.
Small, semi-double flowers of 20 petals, pompon shape; clear crimson in colour. Slight fragrance. Light glossy foliage.

A late flowering variety—end of July. A rampant grower, excellent for arches, trellis, pergolas, also as a weeping standard.

Cyclamen. (166) FLORI. DELBARD 1961. (Frau Karl Druschki × Orange Triumph) × Tonnere.
Blooms of 12 petals, 3 in. across when open, freely produced. Cyclamen pink. Slight fragrance. Foliage small dark green and plentiful. Vigorous. 2 ft. 6 in.

Cynthia Brooke. (333) H.T. MCGREDY 1943. Le Progress × (Mme. Melanie Soupert × Le Progress).
Large double globular flowers; empire yellow, reverse light salmon. Fruity fragrance. Dark leathery foliage. Growth bushy and robust. 2 ft.

Daily Sketch. (163) FLORI. H.T. type McGredy 1960. Ma Perkins × Grand Gala.
Blooms full and shapely 3½ in. across, produced in singly and in clusters. Pink and silver bi-colour. Fragrant. Deep green foliage. Vigorous. 2 ft. 6 in.

Dairy Maid. (64) FLORI. E.B. LE GRICE 1957. (Poulsen's Pink × Ellinor Le Grice) × Mrs. Pierre S. du Pont.
Blooms single, cream fading to white, buds yellow splashed carmine. Growth moderately vigorous. 2 ft.

Dame de Coeur. (18) H.T. LOUIS LENS 1959. Peace × Independence.
Large full dusky pink flowers. Slight fragrance. Vigorous. 2 ft. 6 in.

Danse du Feu. (395) CL. MALLERIN 1954. Paul's Scarlet Climber × unnamed R. multiflora seedling.
Flowers scarlet red, medium sized, double 30-35 petals, opening flat. Fragrant. A vigorous repeat flowering climber. Very hardy. Syn. Spectacular.

Danse des Sylphes. (382) CLIMBER. MALLERIN 1957. Danse du Feu × Toujours.
Blooms bright orange red, medium size and cupped produced in clusters. Recurrent bloom. A vigorous climber. 10-12 ft. For wall or pillar.

Dany Robin. (215) FLORI. MEILLAND 1959. Goldilocks × Fashion.
Salmon shaded soft peach. Blooms large, full and freely produced in trusses. Moderately vigorous up to 2 ft.

Day of Triumph (72) See Rendez-vous.

Dearest. (65) FLORI. A. DICKSON 1960. Seedling × Spartan.
Large cupped and flat of 30 petals. Clear pink. Very sweet fragrance. Dark green foliage. Growth robust and branching. Approx. 2 ft.

Detroiter (86) See Brilliant

Diablotin. (296) FLORI. GEORGES DELBARD 1961. Orleans Rose × Fashion.
Blooms cupped 16 small petals, 2 in. across when open produced in large trusses. Geranium red, slightly fragrant. Foliage dark green and plentiful. Growth strong and branching. 3 ft.

Diamant. (336) FLORI. R. KORDES 1962. Korona × Spartan.
Blooms small, 2 in. across, full petalled, produced in trusses. Orange red. Faint fragrance. Foliage large deep green. Growth erect and vigorous. 3 ft.

Diamond Jubilee. (63) H.T. BOERNER 1947. Marechal Niel × Feu Pernet-Ducher.
Large full flowers of 25-30 petals. Buff-yellow. Very fragrant. Leathery foliage. A first class variety in a good season. Growth vigorous. 2 ft. to 2 ft. 6 in.

Dickson's Flame. (216) FLORI. DICKSON 1958. Independence seedling × Nymph.
Large, semi-double 12 petals, scarlet-flame flowers. Slight fragrance. Dwarf growth 18 in. Blooms hold their colour well, but inclined to hang down.

Display. (188) FLORI. ARNOT 1956. Orange Triumph × Spek's Yellow.
Well formed medium sized, semi-double flowers; salmon-pink turning to cherry pink. Slight fragrance. Produced in large clusters. Glossy bronze-green foliage. 3 ft.

Donald Prior. (253) FLORI. PRIOR 1938. Unnamed seedling × D.T. Poulsen.
Bright scarlet flowers, large, semi-double, cup shaped. Fragrant. Produced in large clusters. Dark leathery foliage. Vigorous. 3 ft.

Doreen. (261) H.T. ROBINSON 1951. Lydia × McGredy's Sunset.
Flowers deep golden orange flushed scarlet; well formed. Dark foliage. Growth moderate. 2 ft.

Dorothy Anderson. (270) H.T. MCGREDY 1940. Sam McGredy × George Dickson.
Flowers large and full of 33 petals, high-centred; colour light pink. Slight fragrance. At its best a fine rose, but susceptible to weather damage. Vigorous up to 2 ft. 6 in.

Dorothy Peach. (271) H.T. ROBINSON 1957. Lydia × Peace.
Large full high-centred flowers of 37 petals; deep yellow flushed pink in colour. Fragrant. Dark glossy foliage. Growth robust and branching 2 ft. 6 in.

Dorothy Wheatcroft. (165) SHRUB. TANTAU 1960.
Medium sized, semi-double blooms of 17 petals, 2½ in. across when open produced in large clusters. Bright orient red overlaid blood red. Slight fragrance. Large bright green foliage. Growth very tall and upright. 4 ft. Suitable for back row or the border.

Dortmund. (372) KORDESII CLIMBER. KORDES 1955. Seedling × R. kordesii. Flowers red with white eye; very large single and open. Fragrant. Produced in large clusters. A rampant grower, repeat flowering, which makes a fine pillar rose.

Dr. Debat. (28) H.T. MEILLAND 1948. Blooms large, full and high-centre of 25-30 petals; bright pink shaded coral. Fragrant. Vigorous. 3 ft. 6 in., but rather a sparse bloomer. Syn. La Rosee.

Dr. Faust. (41) See Faust.

Dr. W. van Fleet. (403) R. VAN FLEET 1910. R. wichuraiana × Safrano) × Souv. du Pres. Carnot.
Blooms full, medium size shapely in bud opening flat. Cameo pink fading to flesh-white. Very fragrant. Dark glossy small foliage. A rampant profuse summer flowering variety, which requires little pruning as it flowers on the old wood.

Dr. A. J. Verhage. (159) H.T. VERBEEK 1961. Tawny Gold × (Baccara × seedling).
Bright yellow blooms, full and shapely. Fragrant. Foliage dark green. Moderately vigorous. 2 ft.

Dreamland. (95) FLORI. TANTAU 1959. Medium sized, double blooms 20 petals of soft peach pink colouring.

Slight fragrance. Vigorous and bushy. 2 ft. Syn. Traumland.

Dries Verschuren. (325) H.T. VERSCHUREN 1961. Geheimrat Duisberg × seedling.
Blooms of two tone yellow, inside of petal pale yellow, reverse buttercup yellow. Full, shapely and large. Foliage shiny dark bronze green. Growth robust up to 2 ft. 6 in.

Duet. (6) H.T. ARMSTRONG 1960. Fandango × Roundelay.
Crimson flowers with lighter reverse. Well formed, moderately large and full. Fragrant. Leathery foliage. Vigorous. 2 ft. 6 in.

Dusky Maiden. (191) FLORI. LE GRICE 1947. (Daily Mail Scented Rose × Etoile de Hollande) × Else Poulsen.
Large, single blackish crimson-scarlet flowers. Very fragrant. Dwarf but robust growth up to 2 feet.

Dwarf King. (418) MIN. KORDES 1957. World's Fair × Tom Thumb.
Flowers small, full, opening flat. Carmine. Fragrant. Produced in small clusters. Foliage glossy. Dwarf growth 8 to 10 in. Syn. Zwergkonig.

Eden Rose. (73) H.T. MEILLAND 1953. Peace × Signora.
Flowers deep pink with lighter reverse. Large full 55-60 petals and very fragrant. Dark green glossy foliage. A very tall upright grower. 3 ft. 6 in.

El Capitan. (36) FLORI. ARMSTRONG 1959. Charlotte Armstrong × Floradora.
Large and full, high centred. Cherry red in colour. Slight fragrance. Glossy, leathery foliage. Vigorous. 2 ft. 6 in.

Elegance. (391) L.F.C. BROWNELL 1937.
Glenn Dale × (Mary Wallace × Miss Lilita Armour).
Medium size shapely, full petalled flowers; yellow fading to white at edges. Fragrant. Dark glossy foliage. Repeat flowering. A moderately vigorous climber. 10 ft.

Ellinor le Grice. (78) H.T. LE GRICE 1949. Lilian × Golden Dawn.
Clear yellow, large, full and globular with 50 petals. Pleasant fruity fragrance. Dark glossy leathery foliage. Growth vigorous and compact. 2 ft.

Elmshorn. (360) SHRUB. KORDES 1951. Hamburg × Verdun.
Deep pink flowers; small full 20 petals, cupped (pompon shape). Slight fragrance. Produced in large trusses. Glossy light green foliage. Long stems, but rather straggly. 6 ft.

Elsa Arnot. (228). H.T. CROLL 1958. Ena Harkness × Peace.
Yellow, inside petals pink to red. Blooms large and full. Very fragrant. Growth vigorous and upright. 3 ft.

Elysium. (45) FLORI. KORDES 1960.
Large full flowers of 30-40 petals. Light salmon in colour. Freely produced. Sweet fragrance. Growth tall with plentiful glossy mid-green foliage. 2 ft. 6 in.

Embrasement. (314) FLORI. CHABERT 1956.
Fiery red blooms, double, produced in clusters of 8-12. Bronzy foliage. Vigorous. 3 ft.

Emily. (272) H.T. BAINES 1949. Mme. Butterfly × Mrs. Henry Bowles.
Blooms very large and full, 40 petals, shapely. Soft rose pink. Fragrant. Vigorous. 2 ft. 6 in.

Emily Gray. (390) R. WILLIAMS 1918.
Jersey Beaty × Countess du Cayla.
Shapely buds golden yellow opening to buff yellow. Medium size blooms produced in large trusses. Summer flowering. Foliage small, dark and glossy. Vigorous but inclined to die-back. 15 ft.

Ena Harkness. (211) H.T. NORMAN 1946. Crimson Glory × Southport.
Crimson scarlet flowers freely produced, large, full and high centred. Very fragrant. Leathery foliage. Vigorous up to 2 ft. 6 in., makes an excellent standard.

Enterprise. (102) FLORI. KORDES 1957. Masquerade × seedling.
Flowers deep pink edged peach; medium sized and semi-double of 20 petals. Fragrant. Produced in large clusters. Dark glossy foliage. Vigorous and upright. 2 ft. 6 in.

Erfurt. (356) SHRUB. KORDES 1939.
Eva × Reveil Dijonnais.
Blooms very large, semi-double, citron yellow edged carmine. Very fragrant. Foliage bronzy and wrinkled. Recurrent bloom. Vigorous up to 6 ft.

Estrellita de Oro (420) See Baby Gold Star.

Ethel Sanday. (268) H.T. MEE 1954.
Rex Anderson × Audrey Cobden.
Well formed flowers, large and full—34 petals. Yellow flushed apricot at base. Slight fragrance. Dark green foliage. Vigorous and branching, 2 ft. 6 in.

Evelyn Fison. (173) FLORI. MCGREDY 1961. Moulin Rouge × Korona.
Blooms of brilliant scarlet, 3 in. when open, produced in well spaced trusses. 29 small petals. Slight fragrance. Foliage small, medium green. Habit compact and bushy. 2 ft. 6 in.

Excelsa (402) R. WALSH, 1909.
Bright crimson flowers in full large clusters; very vigorous with free summer flowering. This still remains one of the best ramblers.

Fandango. (101) H.T. SWIM 1950.
Charlotte Armstrong × unnamed seedling.
Bud turkey-red base yellow; large orange-red double flowers of 16-25 petals. A striking colour. Dark leathery glossy green foliage. Growth vigorous and upright. 2 ft. 6 in.

Fanfare. (96) FLORI. SWIM 1956.
Fandango × Pinocchio.
Large double flowers of 20-30 petals, coral to orange-red with yellow reverse. Produced in large clusters. Fragrant. Leathery glossy foliage. Growth vigorous and spreading. 2 ft.

Fanny Blankers-Koen. (180) H.T.
Verschuren-Pechtold 1949. Talisman × unnamed seedling.
Blooms semi-double shapely in bud opening flat. Very fragrant. Orange yellow flushed and veined red. Glossy foliage. Growth upright and robust. 2 ft. 6 in.

Fantan. (319) H.T. MEILLAND 1958.
(Pigalle × Prelude) × self.
Large, full cupped flowers of 40-55 petals. Burnt-orange to yellow-ochre in colour. Slight fragrance. Leathery foliage. Moderately vigorous. 2 ft.

Fantasia. (82) H.T. DICKSON 1943.
Seedling × Lord Lonsdale.
Blooms double and open, medium size. Yellow fading to cream towards edges of petals. Fragrant. Foliage glossy. Growth vigorous and bushy. 2 ft. to 2 ft. 6 in.

Farandole. (117) FLORI. MEILLAND 1959. (Goldilocks × Moulin Rouge) × (Goldilocks × Fashion).
Semi-double well formed flowers, light vermilion in colour. Produced in large trusses. Growth uniform of medium height. 2 ft.

Fascinating. (24) H.T. GLADYS FISHER 1960.
Blooms medium size, full petalled (25) short in centre, a combination of crimson and yellow with yellow reverse. Slight fragrance. Large glossy foliage. Growth dwarf and bushy. 2 ft.

Fashion. (161) FLORI. BOERNER 1949.
Pinocchio × Crimson Glory.
Bud deep peach opening to full medium sized blooms 3 in. across, coral salmon, produced in clusters. Fragrant. Growth vigorous and bushy. 3 ft.

Faust. (41) FLORI. KORDES 1957.
Masquerade × Spek's Yellow.
Medium sized double flowers of 25 petals. Golden yellow shaded orange-pink. Fragrant. Produced in very large clusters. Dark glossy foliage. Growth very tall and upright. 3 ft. 6 in. to 4 ft. Syn. Dr. Faust.

Fervid. (294) FLORI. LE GRICE 1960.
Pimpernell × Korona.
Blooms almost single, cupped, 3 in. across produced in clusters. Scarlet orange. Slight fragrance. Foliage dark green and large. Growth bushy and vigorous. 3 ft.

Feurio. (203) FLORI. KORDES 1955.
Rudolph Timm × Independence.
Medium sized full blooms of 30 petals, orange scarlet in colour. Slight fragrance. Glossy bright green foliage. Dwarf bushy growth. 1 ft. 6 in. to 2 ft.

Firecracker. (245) FLORI. BOERNER 1956. Pinocchio seedling × Numa Fay seedling.
Large semi-double flowers 12-15 petals; brilliant scarlet with yellow base. Light green leathey foliage. Bushy growth. 2 ft.

Fire King. (121) FLORI. MEILLAND 1959. Moulin Rouge × Fashion.
High centred, medium sized flowers, 45 petals, scarlet in colour. Musk fragrance. Dark green leathery foliage. Vigorous. 2 ft. 6 in.

First Choice. (279) FLORI. MORSE 1958. Masquerade × Sultane.
Large single fiery orange-scarlet flowers with yellow centre. Fragrant. Makes a large bush up to 4 ft.

First Love. (53) H.T. SWIM 1952. Charlotte Armstrong × Show Girl. Pale pink shaded with deeper tints, full 25-30 petals, blooms of medium size. Fragrant. Vigorous and bushy. 3 ft. A good cut flower variety.

F. J. Grootendorst. (373) SHRUB. DE GOEY 1918. R. rugosa rubra × unknown polyantha.
Bright red flowers, small double open, petals serrated at edges. Slight fragrance. Small, dark leathery foliage. Growth vigorous and bushy 5-6 ft. Makes a good hedge or specimen plant.

Flamenco. (81) FLORI. MCGREDY 1960. Tantau's Triumph × Spartan.
Full flowers, 21 petals, opening flat. Salmon red with lighter reverse. Slight fragrance. Dark green foliage. Vigorous upright growth. 3 ft.

Flammentanz. (254) CLR. KORDES 1955. Johannes Bottner × rubiginosa magnifica.
Blooms fiery red with velvety blush, full, produced in trusses. Growth vigorous. A hardy climber up to 15 ft.

Flaming Sunset. (181) H.T. EDDIE 1948. Sport of McGredy's Sunset.
Blooms large, full and shapely. Deep orange reverse yellow. Bronzy light green foliage. Moderate growth. 2 ft.

Florence Mary Morse. (118) FLORI. KORDES 1951. Baby Chateau × Magnifica.
Large semi-double flowers, 15 petals, copper scarlet in colour. Produced in large trusses. Dark glossy foliage. Vigorous and bushy. 3 ft. Excellent for a low hedge.

Florida von Scharbeutz. (11) FLORI. Hybrid tea type. KORDES 1957. Spek's Yellow × seedling.
Blooms large, double 20-25 petals, high centred, borne in trusses. Orange salmon. Moderate fragrance. Growth vigorous and upright. 2 ft. 6 in.

Foetida. (350) (R. LUTEA) SHRUB.
Flowers single 2½ in. in diameter; bright yellow with sickly sweet odour. Rich green foliage. Semi-vigorous. 4 to 5 ft.

Forty-Niner. (329) H.T. SWIM 1949. Contrast × Charlotte Armstrong.
Blooms large, 30-40 petals, slightly fragrant. Bi-colour, light crimson with gold reverse. Glossy green foliage. Vigorous. 2 ft. 6 in.

Frau Karl Druschki. (315) H.T. LAMBERT 1901. Merveille de Lyon × Mme. Caroline Testout.
Pointed bud tinged carmine-pink; developing into very large, double open flowers snow white with the centre occasionally blush-pink. Faint fragrance. Vigorous. 3 ft.

Fred Howard. (109) H.T. HOWARD 1952. Pearl Harbour × unnamed seedling. High centred large flowers, 50 petals, golden orange shaded pink. Slight fragrance. Growth very tall and slender. 4 ft.

Fred Streeter. (7) H.T. KORDES 1955. Luis Brinas × Spek's Yellow. Well formed flowers clear yellow in colour; large, 48 petals. Fragrant. Dark green foliage. Vigorous and upright. 2 ft. 6 in.

Frensham. (171) FLORI. NORMAN 1946. Seedling × Crimson Glory. Deep scarlet crimson, semi-double, 3 in. across produced in large clusters. Very free and continuous. Very vigorous and branching. Suitable for hedge. 4 ft.

Friedrich Heyer. (303) SHRUB. TANTAU 1956. Large bright orange flowers, 10 petals. Fragrant. Produced in large clusters. Dark green glossy foliage. Growth vigorous and upright. 3 ft.

Fritz Thiedemann. (337) H.T. TANTAU 1960. Buds red opening to deep vermilion. Blooms large 4 in., full and shapely. Growth vigorous and compact 2 ft. to 2 ft. 6 in.

Frühlingsanfang. (342) SHRUB. KORDES 1950. Joanna Hill × R. spinosissima altaica. Blooms single and large; ivory white. Slight fragrance. Foliage glossy. Growth vigorous and bushy up to 8 ft.

Frühlingsduft. (343) SHRUB. KORDES 1948. Joanna Hill × R. spinosissima altaica. Flowers large, full, opening flat. Lemon yellow flushed light pink and apricot. Very fragrant. Summer flowering. Growth vigorous and bushy up to 5 ft.

Frühlingsgold. (341 and 351) SHRUB. KORDES 1937. Joanna Hill × R. spinosissima hispida. Nasturtium red bud developing into golden yellow flower; large, single and open. Very fragrant. Large light soft foliage with wrinkled appearance. Growth vigorous up to 8 ft. with long arching stems. Early summer flowering.

Frühlingsmorgen. (344) SHRUB. KORDES 1942. (E.G. Hill × Catherine Kordes) × Rosa spinosissima altaica. Blooms single, medium size produced in large trusses. Cherry pink shaded yellow at base with maroon stamens. Summer flowering only, large maroon heps in Autumn. Vigorous. 5 ft.

Gail Borden. (274) H.T. KORDES 1957. R.M.S. Queen Mary × Viktoria Adelheid. Pale orange-yellow bud developing into deep rose-pink flowers with chrome yellow base reverse lighter; very large, 50-55 petals, and high centred. Fragrant. Dark glossy leathery foliage. Vigorous and branching. 2 ft. 6 in.

Garden Party. (48) H.T. ARMSTRONG 1959. Charles Armstrong × Peace. Ivory to cream tinged pink; large and full loose formation, 35 petals. Slight fragrance. Abundant normal green foliage. Habit vigorous and bushy. 3 ft 6 in.

Garten Zauber. (57) H.T. KORDES 1961. Independence × Montezuma. Shapely blooms, medium size, and full petalled. Slight fragrance. Orange scarlet. Growth vigorous. 2 ft. 6 in.

Garvey. (149) H.T. MCGREDY 1960. McGredy's Yellow × Karl Herbst. Globular well formed flowers of 30 petals, 6 in. across when open. Pale geranium-lake. Moderate fragrance. Light green foliage. Growth vigorous and upright. 2 ft. 6 in.

Gay Lady. (108) H.T. SWIM 1953. Charlotte Armstrong × Piccaninny. Large full blooms 4 in. across, currant red. Spicy fragrance. Foliage dark and glossy. Growth vigorous and upright. 3 ft. 6 in.

Gay Vista. (366) SHRUB. RIETHMULLER 1957. Blooms large, light pink, produced in clusters. Repeat flowering. Moderate growth up to 3 ft. 6 in.

Gentle. (107) FLORI. LENS 1960. Independence × (Lady Sylvia × Fashion). Flowers medium sized and double, 18-25 petals; salmon pink. Fragrant. Growth compact and bushy. 2 ft.

Gertrude Gregory. (221) H.T. GREGORY 1957. Sport of Lady Belper. Bright golden yellow flowers; large double and high centred. Fragrant. Dark glossy foliage. Growth robust and bushy. 2 ft.

Gioia (184) See Peace.

Gipsy Boy (365) See Zigeuner Knabe.

Gloire de Dijon. (413) CL.T. JACOTOT 1853. Unknown Tea × Souv. de la Malmaison. Flowers rich buff pink shaded orange towards the centre; very large and full. Recurrent bloom. Fragrant. A rampant climber suitable for wall.

Gloria Dei (184) See Peace

Gloria Mundi (224) POLY.POM. DE RUITER 1929. Sport of Superb. Flowers small and double, brilliant orange-scarlet in colour, produced in clusters. Light glossy foliage. Growth bushy. 18 in.

Gold Crown. (15) H.T. KORDES 1960. Peace × Spek's Yellow. Large full flowers; deep yellow in colour. Glossy foliage. Very tall sturdy growth up to 3 ft. 6 in. Best suited for border. Syn. Goldkrone.

Gold Cup. (189) FLORI. BOERNER 1957. Goldilocks seedling × King Midas seedling. Large, flat double flowers, 25-30 petals; produced in clusters. Golden yellow. Fragrant. Dark glossy foliage. Bushy growth. 2 ft.

Golden Dawn. (1) H.T. GRANT 1929. Elegante × Ethel Somerset. Pale buff yellow to cream; blooms large and shapely, though many are inclined to quarter, 45 petals. Good fragrance. Leathery large foliage. Growth vigorous. 2 ft.

Golden Giant. (258) H.T. KORDES 1960. Blooms moderate sized, full, 45 petals; bright clear yellow. Slight fragrance. Light green foliage. Growth lanky. 4 ft. Unsuitable for formal beds. Syn. Gold Rausch.

Golden Jewel. (98) FLORI. TANTAU 1959. Medium sized full flowers produced in trusses. Golden yellow. Dark green glossy foliage. Dwarf branching growth up to 2 ft.

Golden Masterpiece. (135) H.T. BOERNER 1954. Mandalay × Spek's Yellow. Very large flowers well shaped and high-centred, 35 petals. Lemon yellow. Fragrant. Glossy foliage. Vigorous and upright. 2 ft. 6 in.

Golden Melody. (14) H.T. LA FLORIDA 1934. Mme. Butterfly × (Lady Hillingdon × Souv. de Claudius Pernet).
Yellow bud opening to light buff flower, changing to cream tinged pink with age; very large well formed blooms of 35 petals. Very fragrant. Growth vigorous though foliage rather coarse. 2 ft. 6 in. Syn. Irene Churruca.

Golden Sceptre (218) See Spek's Yellow.

Golden Showers. (363) SHRUB or SEMI-CLIMBER. LAMMERTS 1956. Charlotte Armstrong × Capt. Thomas.
Daffodil-yellow flowers, large double high centred opening flat 25-30 petals. Recurrent bloom. Produced singly and in clusters. Fragrant. Dark glossy foliage. Makes a good shrub or pillar rose.

Goldilocks. (100) FLORI. BOERNER 1945. Unnamed seedling × Dubloons.
Medium sized globular flowers of 45 petals; deep yellow in colour fading to cream with age. Glossy leathery foliage. Growth vigorous and bushy. 2 ft.

Goldkrone (15) See Gold Crown.

Gold Marie. (255) FLORI. KORDES 1958. Masquerade × Golden Main.
Flowers orange-gold; very large and semi-double, 15-20 petals frilled at edges. Strong fragrance. Produced in clusters. Glossy foliage. Vigorous and branching. 2 ft.

Gold Rausch (258) See Golden Giant.

Gordon Eddie. (275) H.T. EDDIE 1949. Royal Visit × Cynthia Brooke.
Flowers deep apricot with lighter edges. Very large and full, 40 petals.

Fragrant. Glossy leathery foliage. Vigorous and bushy. 2 ft. Subject to black spot.

Grace de Monaco. (281) H.T. MEILLAND 1956. Peace × Michele Meilland.
Very large globular flowers, light rose pink. Very fragrant. Leathery foliage. Strong and upright. 2 ft. 6 in.

Grand Gala. (324) H.T. MEILLAND 1954. Peace × Independence.
Bi-colour rose red reverse of petals white overshaded pale pink; Large, high-centred, 45-50 petals. Slight fragrance. Leathery foliage. 2 ft.

Grand Master. (359) SHRUB. KORDES 1954. Sangerhausen × Sunmist.
Flowers large and flat, semi-double, apricot shaded buff and orange. Fragrant. A moderate constitution. Will make a straggly bush up to 4-5 ft.

Grandmère Jenny. (397 and 398) H.T. CLIMBER. MEILLAND 1955. Peace × (Julien Potin × Sensation).
Large double attractive loose flowers, apricot yellow in colour edged and suffused pink. Dark glossy foliage. Slight fragrance. Strong and bushy. 3 ft. in bush form. The climbing form makes an excellent pillar rose.

Grey Pearl. (33) H.T. MCGREDY 1945. (Mrs. Lamplough × seedling) × (Sir David Davis × Southport).
Large double high-centred flowers; lavender-grey shaded olive and tan in colour. Fragrant. Glossy foliage. Vigorous. 2 ft. Syn. The Mouse.

Guinee. (387) CL. H.T. MALLERIN 1938. Souv. de Claudius Denoyel × Ami Quinard.
Blooms deep garnette occasionally mottled scarlet; large and double. Recurrent. Very fragrant. Leathery foliage. A good climber for walls.

Gustav Frahm. (273) SHRUB. KORDES 1958. Fanal × Ama.
Glowing crimson scarlet darker at the edges. Medium sized semi-double blooms of 25 petals. Produced in large trusses. Slight fragrance. Vigorous and upright. 3 ft. 6 in.

Hamburger Phoenix. (409) KORDE-SEMI CLIMBER. KORDES 1954. R. kordesii × seedling.
Large deep red semi-double flowers. Recurrent blooming. Slightly fragrant. Borne in clusters. Dark glossy foliage. An excellent pillar rose.

Hansestadt Bremen. (259) FLORI. KORDES 1958. Ama × Fanal.
Deep salmon pink flowers opening very large and full; produced in clusters. Slightly fragrant. Leathery foliage. Vigorous and bushy. 2 ft. 6 in.

Happiness. (120) H.T. MEILLAND 1951. (Rome Glory × Tassin) × Charles P. Kilham × (Charles P. Kilham × Capucine Chambard).
Very large double flowers of 45-50 petals. Brilliant red turning to crimson-carmine with age. Slight fragrance. Vigorous and upright. 2 ft 6 in. Grown extensively under glass.
Syn. Rouge Meilland.

Happy Anniversary. (172) FLORI. DELBARD 1960. (Incendie × Chic Parisien) × (Floradora × Sondermeldung). Blooms high centred, full, open, produced singly and in clusters. Salmon pink, moderate fragrance. Foliage dark glossy green. Growth vigorous and upright. 3 ft. Syn. Heureux Anniversaire.

Hassan. (238) FLORI. MCGREDY 1961. Tivoli × Independence.
Glowing scarlet. Blooms 4 in. across when open. 28 petals, produced in large clusters. Fragrant. Light green glossy foliage. Vigorous. 2 ft. 6 in.

Hawaii. (88) H.T. BOERNER 1960. Gold Masterpiece × unnamed seedling.
Blooms very large, long and high centred, full. Orange flushed coral. Fragrant. Foliage normal green and leathery. Very vigorous and upright. 3 ft.

Hebe. (247) H.T. DICKSON 1949.
Very large, double, high pointed flowers of 27 petals, rosy salmon suffused orange and apricot yellow. Very fragrant. Glossy bronzy green foliage. Vigorous. 2 ft. 6 in.

Heidelberg. (226) SHRUB. KORDES 1958. Sparrieshoop × World's Fair.
Very large, double flat flowers of bright red colouring. Produced in trusses and recurrent. Fragrant. Dark glossy leathery foliage. Vigorous. 3 ft. 6 in. Suitable for hedging or specimen shrub.

Helen Traubel. (99) H.T. SWIM 1951. Charlotte Armstrong × Glowing Sunset.
Large, double high centred flowers, opening flat; 20-25 petals. Colouring, apricot flushed pink. Fragrant. Leathery, dull green foliage. Vigorous and tall. 3ft. 6in. Blooms inclined to hang down.

Henry Morse. (110) SHRUB. KORDES 1958.
Blooms medium size, semi.-double, produced in large trusses, slightly fragrant. Recurrent. Deep blood red shaded scarlet. Vigorous and branching. 3 ft.

Heureux Anniversaire (172) See Happy Anniversary.

Highlight. (76) FLORI. ROBINSON 1957. Seedling × Independence.
Medium sized double blooms of 24 petals. Orange-scarlet, very bright and intense when young. Fragrant. Produced in large clusters. Vigorous and upright. 2 ft. 6 in.

High Noon. (225) CL. H.T. LAMMERTS 1946. Soeur Thérèse × Capt. Thomas.
Medium sized double blooms of 25-30 petals. Lemon-yellow flushed red. Recurrent bloom. Rich spicy fragrance. Glossy leathery foliage. Growth moderate, best as pillar rose.

High Society. (87) H.T. KORDES 1961. Blooms high pointed and double, 30 petals. Glowing red. Slight fragrance. Medium green foliage. Vigorous and bushy. 2 ft.

Hollanderin (113) See Red Favourite.

Honeymoon. (44) FLORI. KORDES 1960. Claire Grammerstorf × Spek's Yellow.
Medium sized double blooms of miniature H.T. shape in bud, opening flat. Canary yellow. Slight fragrance. Heavily veined dark green foliage. Vigorous and bushy. 2 ft.

Hugh Dickson. (414) H.P. H. DICKSON 1905. Lord Bacon × Grüss an Teplitz.
Very large globular blooms of 38 petals. Rich crimson shaded scarlet. Very fragrant and recurrent. Growth vigorous and upright, and best grown as semi-climber. Unsuitable for formal beds.

Huntsman. (278) H.T. H. ROBINSON 1951. The Queen Alexandra Rose seedling × Crimson Glory.
Large double flowers of 35-40 petals, bi-colour spectrum red with yellow reverse. Fragrant. Dark foliage. Moderately vigorous. 2 ft.

Iceberg. (42) FLORI. KORDES 1958. Robin Hood × Virgo.
Large double flat flowers of pure white colouring. Freely produced in large trusses. Fragrant. Light green foliage. Vigorous and branching. 2. ft. 6 in.
Syn. Schneewittchen.

Independence. (210) FLORI. KORDES 1951. Crimson Glory × Baby Chateau.
Medium sized double flowers, cupped, of 35 petals; pure scarlet with blackish outer petals. Vigorous. 2 ft. 6 in.
Syn. Kordes Sondermeldung. Syn. Reina Elisenda.

Invitation. (23) H.T. SWIM AND WEEKS 1961. Charlotte Armstrong × Signora.
Blooms medium size and high centred, double. Rich salmon pink, base yellow. Abundant medium green foliage. Growth vigorous and upright. 2 ft. 6 in.

Irene Churruca (14) See Golden Melody

Isobel Harkness. (250) H.T. NORMAN 1957. Phyllis Gold × McGredy's Yellow.
Deep yellow. Slight fragrance. Blooms small and shapely, freely produced. Growth vigorous and branching up to 2 ft. 6 in.

Isabel de Ortiz. (205) H.T. KORDES 1961. Peace × Perfecta.
Blooms full and well formed of 52 petals, 5½ in. across when open. Deep pink with silver reverse. Fragrant. Foliage dark green and glossy. Vigorous and upright. 3 ft.

Ivory Fashion. (148) FLORI. BOERNER 1958. Sonata × Fashion.

Large, semi-double flowers, ivory white produced in large clusters. Fragrant. Leathery foliage. Growth vigorous. 3 ft.

Jane Lazenby. (204) FLORI. MCGREDY 1958. Alain × Mme. Henri Guillot. Blooms shapely in bud, opening flat 3 in., 25 petals. Produced in clusters. Carmine pink with yellow eye. Slight fragrance. Large dark green foliage. Vigorous. 2 ft. 6 in.

Jiminy Cricket. (198) FLORI. BOERNER 1954. Goldilocks × Geranium Red. Tangerine red bud opening to coral-orange to pink-coral blooms; medium size and double, cupped shaped 25-30 petals. Fragrant. Glossy foliage. Vigorous and branching. 2 ft.

John S. Amstrong. (49) H.T. ARMSTRONG 1961. Charlotte Armstrong × unnamed seedling. Blooms large and flat of 48 petals produced freely on good stiff stems. Attractive colouring, rich scarlet crimson. Slight fragrance. Foliage dark green and plentiful. A vigorous variety of good habit. 2 ft. 6 in.

Jolie Madame. (320) H.T. MEILLAND 1959. (Independence × Happiness) × Better Times. Blooms medium size, full and cupped. Bright rose. Slight fragrance. Medium green foliage. Growth vigorous and upright. Produced for glass houses and cut flower trade.

Josephine Bruce. (308) H.T. BEES 1949. Crimson Glory × Madge Whipp. Large high pointed double flowers, 24 petals. Deep crimson. Fragrant. Dark foliage Vigorous and branching. 2 ft. 6 in.

June Bride. (138) FLORI. SHEPHERD 1957. (Mme. Butterfly × New Dawn) × Crimson Glory. Blooms large 30 petals, high centred and fragrant. Creamy white clusters of 3-12. Foliage large and leathery. Vigorous. 3 ft.

June Opie. (153) FLORI. KORDES 1958. Masquerade × Seedling. Blooms semi-double, 3 in. across, produced in trusses. Apricot shaded salmon pink. Slight fragrance. Growth vigorous and upright. 3 ft.

June Park. (209) H.T. PARK 1958. Peace × Crimson Glory. Large well shaped blooms of 40 petals. Clear rose-pink. Very fragrant. Dark foliage. Growth vigorous but sprawling. 2 ft.

Karen Poulsen. (199) FLORI. S. POULSEN 1933. Kirsten Poulsen × Veruvius. Single flowers of a brilliant scarlet colour, showing golden stamens. Produced in large trusses. Vigorous. 2 ft.

Karl Herbst. (20) H.T. KORDES 1950. Independence × Peace. Large, well shaped. Red with lighter reverse. Slightly fragrant. Very free flowering and a splendid variety in a good season. Vigorous 3 ft.

Kassel. (370) SHRUB or SEMI-CLIMBER. KORDES 1957. Obergartner Wiebicke × Independence. Large semi-double flowers; scarlet red in colour. Recurrent blooms in trusses. Slightly fragrant. Dark, glossy foliage. Can be grown either as shrub or semi-climber on pillar.

Kathleen Ferrier. (123) SHRUB. BUISMAN 1952. Gartenstolz × Shot Silk. Medium sized semi-double blooms, 18 petals. Deep salmon-pink. Fragrant.

Dark glossy foliage. Very upright and vigorous. 3 ft. Will make an excellent hedging variety.

King's Ransom. (146) H.T. MOREY 1961. Golden Masterpiece × Lydia.
Blooms full, medium size, shapely with high centre. Clear golden yellow. Slight fragrance. Foliage large and glossy. Growth vigorous. 3 ft.

Kleopatra. (90) See Cleopatra.

Köln am Rhein. (381) CLIMBER. KORDES 1956. R. Kordesii × Golden Glow.
Blooms deep pink, large, full and loose, produced in clusters. Repeat flowering. Fragrant. Foliage dark green and glossy. Vigorous. 8 ft. A good pillar rose or large shrub.

Konrad Adenauer. (335) H.T. TANTAU 1955. Crimson Glory × Hens Verschuren.
Large and double, cupped; carmine-red. Very fragrant. Light green glossy foliage. Moderately vigorous. 2 ft.

Kordes Perfecta (16) See Perfecta.

Kordes Sondermeldung (210) See Independence

Korona. (111) FLORI. KORDES 1955.
Medium sized semi-double blooms of 20 petals. Produced in large trusses. Orange-scarlet. Slight fragrance. A variety which at times has peculiar blackish markings on foliage and stems. Vigorous. 2 ft. 6 in.

Lady Belper. (208) H.T. VERSCHUREN 1948.
Large, double and high centred, 38 petals. Coppery-orange shaded light orange. Fragrant. Glossy dark foliage. Growth dwarf and branching. 2 ft.

Lady Elgin. (251) See Thais.

Lady Gay. (408) R. WALSH 1905. R. wichuraiana × Bardou Job.
Small full petalled blooms produced in large clusters. Rich rose pink. Fragrant. Summer flowering only. Very vigorous. 12-20 ft.

Lady Maysie Robinson. (174) H.T. KORDES 1956. Seedling × Peace.
Large double cupped flowers; deep pink with silvery reverse. Fragrant. Dark glossy foliage. Strong growth. 2 ft. 6 in. to 3 ft.

Lady Sonia. (374) SHRUB. MATTOCK 1960. Grandmaster × Doreen.
Medium sized semi-double flowers of 20 petals, 4 in. across when open. Deep golden yellow. Slight fragrance. A lovely free flowering bushy shrub up to 4 ft.

Lady Sylvia. (249) H.T. W. STEVENS 1926. Sport of Mme Butterfly.
Blooms full petalled, high centred and shapely. Deep pink suffused apricot. Fragrant. Growth vigorous, blooms produced on long stems. 3 ft.

Lady Waterlow. (410) CL. H.T. G. NABONNAND 1903. La France × Mme Marie Lavalley.
Blooms large and full; salmon pink edged carmine. Fragrant. Moderately vigorous. 8 to 10 ft.

Lady Zia. (305) H.T. PARK 1959. Peace × Independence.
Very full, 50 petals, well formed high centred flowers. Red flushed orange and scarlet. Slight fragrance. Large dark green glossy foliage, practically evergreen. Vigorous and branching. 2 ft. 6 in.

La Jolie. (252) H.T. BUYL FRERES 1956. Kordes Sondermeldung × Princesse Liliane.

Well formed blooms with 30-35 petals; brilliant geranium red in colour with light green foliage. Upright growth to approx. 2 ft.

La Jolla. (196) H.T. SWIM 1954. Charlotte Armstrong × Contrast.
Large full flowers, 60 petals, high centred; soft pink veined deeper pink with cream and gold centre. Fragrant. Dark glossy foliage. Vigorous and upright. 3 ft.

La Rosee (28) See Dr. Debat.

Lal. (197) H.T. EASLEA 1933. Commonwealth (H.T.) × Florence L. Izzard.
Full blooms of deep salmon-pink colouring, suffused yellow. Very fragrant. Dark foliage. Moderately vigorous. 2 ft.

Lavender Girl. (207) FLORI. MEILLAND 1958. Fantasique × (Ampere × (Charles P. Kilham × Capucine Chambard)).
Blooms medium size, 3 in., full 35-40 petals, cupped, produced in clusters. Fragrant. Magenta changing to lavender. Growth dwarf and bushy. 2 ft.

Lavender Lassie. (195) SHRUB. KORDES 1959.
Blooms rosette shape, medium sized, 65 small petals, lilac pink. Fragrant. Vigorous and bushy. 3 ft. 6 in.

Lavender Pinocchio. (150) FLORI. BOERNER 1948. Pinocchio × Grey Pearl.
Bud chocolate olive brown opening to lavender pink. Blooms full open, 3-3½ in. across, produced in clusters. Foliage leathery. Growth vigorous and bushy. 2 ft. 6 in. to 3 ft.

Leverkussen. (396) KORDESII CLIMBER. KORDES 1955.

Large, semi-double blooms of clear golden yellow colouring. Recurrent bloom. Slightly fragrant. A vigorous pillar rose up to 10 ft.

Liebeslied (30) See Love Song.

Lilac Charm. (175) FLORI. LE GRICE 1961.
Pale lilac mauve with red anthers. Blooms semi-double 12 petals, 3½ in. when open. Fragrant. Mid green foliage. Growth short and bushy up to 2 ft.

Lilac Time. (265) H.T. MCGREDY 1956. Golden Dawn × Luis Brinas.
Blooms full, medium size and shapely lilac. Fragrant. Foliage light green. Growth moderate. 2 ft.

Lilli Marlene. (257) FLORI. KORDES 1959.
Large semi-double blooms, 20 petals, of bright crimson. Produced in large trusses. Slight fragrance. Abundant foliage. Growth vigorous and branching. 2 ft. 6 in.

Love Song. (30) H.T. C. FISHER 1955. Peace × Orange Nassau.
Large full blooms, 45 petals, cupped; Neyron rose, reverse yellow. Very fragrant. Dark glossy foliage. Growth vigorous. 2 ft. 6 in. Syn. Liebeslied.

Lubeck. (330) FLORI. R. KORDES 1962.
Blooms, 25 petals, about 3 in. across when open, produced in large trusses. Orange red. Slight fragrance. Foliage dark green. Growth vigorous and upright. 3 ft. 6 in. to 4 ft.

Lucy Cramphorn. (4) H.T. KRILOFF 1960.
Very full well formed flowers, 5 in. across when open. Turkey red flushed signal red. Fragrant. Glossy foliage. Growth upright and sturdy. 2 ft. 6 in.

Lunelle. (332) F. H.T. MEILLAND 1955. Young France × Signora.
Very large double blooms 50 petals; pale pink in colour. Very fragrant. A vigorous and free blooming variety. 2 ft. 6 in. to 3 ft. Syn. George Sand.

Lydia. (243) H.T. H. ROBINSON 1949. Phyllis Gold × seedling.
Medium sized flowers, full and high centred, bright saffron yellow. Fragrant. Dark, leathery glossy foliage, moderately vigorous. 2 ft.

Magali. (309) H.T. MALLERIN 1952. Charles P. Kilham × Brazier.
Medium sized and full, 45 petals, carmine in colour. Slight fragrance. Abundant leathery foliage. Vigorous and upright. Approx. 2 ft. 6 in.

Magenta. (301) FLORI. KORDES 1954. Yellow floribunda seedling × Lavender Pinocchio. Full flat flowers of medium size, rosy magenta to soft deep mauve. Very fragrant. Dark leathery foliage. Tall, stems inclined to hang down. 3 ft.

Mahagona. (244) H.T. KORDES 1956. Geheimrat Duisberg × Hens Verschuren.
Medium sized open flowers, orange-scarlet with yellow shadings. Fragrant. Leathery foliage. Growth upright and bushy. 2 ft. 6 in.

Maigold. (358) CLIMBER. KORDES 1953. Poulsen's Pink × Fruhlingstag.
Medium size semi-double cupped blooms, 3½ in. across when open; bronze-yellow in colour, very attractive. Very fragrant. Glossy foliage. Flowers early in May and intermittently throughout season if dead heads are removed. Very thorny. An excellent climber or pillar rose up to 10-12 ft.

Ma Perkins. (202) FLORI. BOERNER 1952. Red Radiance × Fashion. Medium sized, globular flowers of 25 petals, produced in small clusters, shell pink, flushed apricot. Fragrant. Rich glossy green foliage. Growth bushy. 2 ft.

Marella. (71) H.T. MEILLAND 1962. Blooms shapely, full and high-centred, deep coral lightened with gold. Slight fragrance. Foliage dark green, glossy. Vigorous; blooms produced on long stems excellent for cutting. 2 ft. 6 in.

Margaret. (304) H.T. DICKSON 1954. May Wettern seedling × Souv. de Denier van der Gon.
Well shaped full blooms of 70 petals; bright pink with silvery pink reverse. Slight fragrance. Free flowering. Growth irregular both sprawly and strong upright stems. 2 ft. 6 in.

Marjorie le Grice. (200) H.T. LE GRICE 1949. Mrs. Sam McGredy × President Plumecocq.
Large full pointed blooms of 30 petals; orange with yellow reverse. Fragrant. Glossy foliage. Vigorous. 2 ft. 6 in.

Masquerade. (70) FLORI. BOERNER 1949. Goldilocks × Holiday.
Small yellow ovoid bud developing into medium sized semi-double flowers; bright yellow turning salmon-pink and then dark red. Especially attractive as several colours appear on one bush at the same time. Slight fragrance. Dark leathery foliage. Vigorous and bushy. 2 ft. 6 in.

McGredy's Ivory. (193) H.T. MCGREDY 1930. Mrs. Charles Lamplough × Mabel Morse.
Very long full flowers (25 – 30 petals) and high centred; ivory white with creamy base. Fragrant. Dark glossy

leathery foliage. Growth vigorous. 2 ft. 6 in.

McGredy's Sunset. (134) H.T. MCGREDY 1936. Margaret McGredy × Mabel Morse.
Full globular flowers opening flat; chrome yellow base shading to scarlet, clear buttercup yellow reverse. Fragrant. Glossy bronze foliage. Moderately vigorous. 2 ft.

McGredy's Yellow. (157) H.T. MCGREDY 1933. Mrs Charles Lamplough × (The Queen Alexandra Rose × J. B. Clark). Blooms large, full and of classic shape. Buttercup yellow. Fragrant. Foliage glossy and bronzy. Growth vigorous but sprawly. 2 ft. 6 in.

Meg. (406) L.F.C. GOSSET 1954. Paul's Lemon Pillar × Mme. Butterfly.
Blooms large, 5½ in., flat, 10 petals, produced in large clusters. Salmon apricot, stamens red. Very attractive. Repeat flowering. Dark glossy foliage. Growth moderately vigorous 8 ft. Suitable for pillar.

Memoriam. (147) H.T. PETERSON & DERING 1960.
Blooms full, shapely and high-centred, white lightly tinged with pink. Fragrant. Foliage mid-green and leathery. Moderately vigorous and compact. 2 ft.

Mermaid. (384) CLR. PAUL 1918. R. bracteata × yellow Tea Rose.
Blooms large, 5-6 in., flat, single, pale sulphur yellow with amber stamens. Fragrant. Repeat flowering. Foliage long slender and dark green. Growth very vigorous up to 30 ft.

Message. (240) H.T. MEILLAND 1956. (Virgo × Peace) × Virgo.

Long, double 28-35 petals and high centred; white faintly shaded cream. Slight fragrance. Light green leathery foliage. Moderately vigorous. 2 ft. Syn. White Knight.

Meteor. (256) FLORI. KORDES 1957. Feurio × Gertrud Westphal.
Large, 3 in. flat and full 40 petals; orange scarlet. Slight fragrance. Abundant light green foliage. Growth moderate. 2 ft.

Michele Meilland. (31) H.T. MEILLAND 1945. Joanna Hill × Peace.
Blooms double, somewhat long and thin, but shapely, freely produced. Slight fragrance. Colour variable, basically salmon rose pink. Growth vigorous. 2 ft. 6 in. to 3 ft.

Milord. (338) H.T. MCGREDY 1962. Rubaiyat × Karl Herbst.
Blooms large, full, urn-shaped and freely produced. Strong fragrance. Foliage dark green. Growth vigorous and upright. 3 ft.

Miracle. (201) FLORI. VERBEEK 1956. Seedling from Fashion.
Medium sized semi-double flowers; orange-salmon. Slight fragrance. Growth vigorous and bushy. 2 ft. 6 in.

Mirandy. (50) H.T. LAMMERTS 1945. Night × Charlotte Armstrong.
Blooms large, globular and full 40-50. petals. Red with dark sheen which blues as blooms age. Foliage leathery. Growth branching, moderately vigorous. 2 ft.

Mischief. (220) H.T. MCGREDY 1961. Peace × Spartan.
Full well formed flowers 4 in. across when open, 25-30 petals. Clear salmon pink with silvery reflexes. Fragrant. Plentiful light green foliage. Vigorous 2 ft. 6 in.

Miss France. (194) FLORI. H.T. type. Gaujard 1955. Peace × Independence. Large and high-centred; coppery cinnabar. Fragrant. Bronze foliage. Vigorous and upright. 2 ft. 6 in.

Miss Ireland. (306) H.T. MCGREDY 1960.
Double well formed flowers; light Dutch vermilion with pale nasturtium orange reverse. Slight fragrance. Deep green foliage. An attactively coloured variety but growth variable and inclined to dieback. 2 ft.

Mme. A. Meilland (184) See Peace.

Clg. Mme. Caroline Testout. (392) CLG. H.T. CHAUVRY 1901. Sport of bush variety introduced by Pernet-Ducher 1890. Mme. de Tartas × Lady Mary Fitzwilliam.
Blooms globular, large and full, satiny rose edge carmine pink. Fragrant. Foliage rich green, soft. A very vigorous reliable climber which is repeat flowering. 20 ft.

Mme Edouard Herriot. (407) CL. H.T. KETTEN BROS. 1921. Climbing sport from bush variety.
Large semi-double blooms; coral-red flushed yellow and bright rosy scarlet, passing to prawn red. Fragrant. Glossy bronzy foliage. Vigorous. 10 ft.

Mme. Henri Guillot. (67) H.T. MALLERIN 1938. Rochefort × unnamed R. foetida bicolour seedling.
Very large shapely urn shaped blooms of 25 petals, orange-coral-red colouring. Slight fragrance. Foliage glossy, large and dark green. In some areas susceptible to Black Spot. Vigorous. 2 ft. 6 in.

Mme. L. Dieudonne. (10) H.T. MEILLAND 1949. (Mme. Joseph Perraud ×

Brazier) × (Charles P. Kilham × Capucine Chambard).
Full large (80 petals) long pointed blooms; rose-red with golden reverse. Fragrant. Dark glossy foliage. Vigorous and bushy. 2 ft.

Mme. Louis. Laperriére. (248) H.T. LAPERRIERE 1951. Crimson Glory × seedling.
Medium sized blooms of good shape; 40-50 petals. Dark foliage, Dark crimson abundantly produced. Growth vigorous and bushy. 2 ft. 6 in.

Mme. Rene. Coty. (300) H.T. MEILLAND 1955. Peace × Brazil.
Blooms, large and full, globular, fragrant. Persian red reverse yellow. Foliage glossy and leathery. Vigorous and upright. 2 ft. 6 in.

Mme. Gregoire Staechelin. (405) CL.H.T. DOT. 1927. Frau Karl Druschki × Chateau de Clos Vougeot.
Large, open, semi-double blooms produced in clusters. Delicate pink stained crimson. Fragrant. Vigorous. 12-14 ft. Summer flowering only.
Syn. Spanish Beauty.

Mojave. (106) H.T. SWIM 1954. Charlotte Armstrong × Signora.
Large flowers of 25 petals with high centre; apricot orange, tinted nasturtium red, veined. Fragrant. A good variety for cutting. Glossy foliage. Growth very upright and tall. 3 ft.

Monique. (242) H.T. PAOLINA 1949. Lady Sylvia × unnamed seedling.
Well shaped, very large full blooms of 25 petals, deep pink on salmon pink base. Very fragrant. Growth vigorous and upright. 2 ft. 6 in.

Montezuma. (22) H.T. SWIM 1955. Fandango × Floradora.

Large full globular blooms with a high centre; plum red in bud, opening to salmon. Inclined to spot from wet. Slight fragrance. Semi-glossy leathery foliage. Very vigorous. 3 ft. 6 in.

Moonbeam. (5) H.T. ROBINSON 1950. Unnamed seedling × McGredy's Yellow.
Large, high centred flowers of deep golden yellow colouring. Fragrant. Dark glossy foliage. Growth moderate and spreading. 2 ft.

Moulin Rouge. (214) FLORI. MEILLAND 1953.
Medium sized 2 in. double blooms of 20-25 petals, cupped in shape. Produced in large clusters. spectrum-red to rose-pink. Slight fragrance. Glossy foliage. Growth upright and bushy. 2 ft. 6 in.

Mrs. Henry Bowles. (68) H.T. CHAPLIN BROS. 1921.
Well shaped large full blooms of 50 petals with high centre; carmine pink flushed salmon. Very fragrant. Dark glossy foliage. Vigorous and bushy. 2 ft. 6 in.

Mrs. Sam McGredy.(145) H.T. MCGREDY 1929. (Donald Macdonald × Golden Emblem) × (seedling × The Queen Alexandra Rose).
Large full flowers; scarlet-copper-orange with reverse heavily flushed red. Fragrant. Reddish bronze glossy foliage. Moderately vigorous and upright. 2 ft. 6 in.

My Choice. (307) H.T. LE GRICE 1958. Wellworth × Ena Harkness.
Lemon yellow suffused scarlet cerise in bud; large full flowers of 30-35 petals, pink with pale yellow reverse when open. Very fragrant. Growth vigorous and branching. 2 ft.

My Fair Lady. (267) FLORI. WHEATCROFT 1959.
Blooms semi-double, 3 in. across when open, produced in trusses. Rose pink flushed deep pink. Slight fragrance. Foliage dark green and plentiful. Growth robust and bushy. 2 ft. 6 in.

My Lady. (69) H.T. ROBINSON 1956. Seedling × Peace.
Large full flowers of 45 petals with high centre; apricot flushed gold. Fragrant. Dark leathery foliage. Vigorous and bushy. 2 ft. 6 in.

Nevada. (340) SHRUB. DOT 1927. La Giralda × R. Moyesii.
Blooms flesh coloured in bud opening creamy white sometimes flushed pink. Almost single, flat and large, 4 in, across. Perpetual flowering. Growth vigorous up to 7 ft. with long arching stems.

New Yorker. (192) H.T. BOERNER 1947. Flambeau × seedling.
Large full blooms with high centre, 35 petals, bright velvety scarlet in colour. Fruity fragrance. Vigorous and bushy. 2 ft. 6 in.

Nocturne. (327) H.T. SWIM 1947. Charlotte Armstrong × Night.
Buds long pointed, flowers cupped and large, 25-28 petals. Cardinal red shaded dark crimson. Growth vigorous and bushy. 2 ft. 6 in.

Nymphenburg. (368) SHRUB. KORDES 1954. Sangerhausen × Sunmist.
Very large, flat, open semi-double blooms, 4 in. across. Salmon-pink shaded orange. Fragrant. Large glossy foliage. Growth vigorous up to 5 ft. A free and continuous flowering shrub.

Ohlala. (297) FLORI. TANTAU 1956. Seedling of Fanal.

Blooms blood red large 3½ in. semi-double and produced in large clusters. Slight fragrance. Foliage dark green and glossy. Growth vigorous. 2 ft. 6 in.

Opera. (276) H.T. GAUJARD 1950. La Belle Irisee × unnamed seedling. Very large double flowers; light scarlet-red with yellow base. Fragrant. Large light green leathery foliage. Habit tall and erect. 3 ft.

Ophelia. (104) H.T. PAUL 1912. Medium sized full shapely blooms; salmon-flesh tinted light yellow in centre. Fragrant. Leathery foliage. Excellent for cutting. Growth branching and vigorous. 2 ft. 6 in.

Orangeade. (299) FLORI. MCGREDY 1959. Orange Sweetheart × Independence. Medium sized semi-double blooms which open flat. Bright deep Dutch vermilion, the young blooms a vivid colour which tone to reddish orange as they fade. Slight fragrance. Growth robust and branching. 2 ft.

Orange Sensation. (80) FLORI. DE RUITER 1960. Medium sized moderately full blooms; bright orange suffused light vermilion towards the edge of the petals. The best yet in the orange shades, retaining its colour well. Sweet fragrance. Deep green foliage abundantly produced. Growth vigorous and branching. 2 ft. 6 in.

Orange Triumph. (124) FLORI. KORDES 1937. Eva × Solarium. Small semi-double blooms; red shaded orange. Slight fragrance. Glossy dark foliage. A very vigorous variety attaining a height of 3 ft. 6 in. to 4 ft.

Ormiston Roy. (355) SHRUB. DORENBOS 1953. R. Spinosissima × R. xanthina. Blooms large, single, deep yellow. Summer flowering only. Growth bushy up to 3 ft.

Paddy McGredy. (206) FLORI. H.T. type. McGredy 1962. Spartan × Tzigane. Medium sized shapely H.T. type blooms of 43 petals produced singly and in trusses. Rose pink. Fragrant. Dark green foliage. Makes a compact bush 2 ft.

Paprika. (116) FLORI. TANTAU 1957. Semi-double bright geranium red blooms, with an attractive bluish ring at base of petals. Very free flowering with handsome dark glossy foliage. A robust uniform growing variety. 2 ft.

Parfum de l'Hay. (378) SHRUB. GRAVEREAUX 1901. (R. damascena × Gen. Jacqueminot) × R. rugosa. Blooms full, globular, produced freely. Repeat bloom. Bright rosy carmine. Very fragrant. Growth vigorous of moderate height, about 4 ft.

Paris-Match. (167) H.T. MEILLAND 1956. Independence × Grand'mére Jenny. Carmine to salmon-pink. Blooms large, full petalled and shapely. Fragrant. Foliage mid-green and leathery. Growth vigorous. 2 ft. 6 in.

Park Direktor Riggers. (177) CLIMBER. KORDES 1957. R. Kordesii × Our Princess. Blooms large semi-double, slight fragrance. Produced in large clusters. Velvety crimson. Foliage dark and glossy. A vigorous climber. 12-15 ft.

Party Dress. (183) H.T. ROBINSON 1961. Gay Crusader × seedling.

Blooms high-centred and large, 5 in. 25 petals. Peach shaded yellow. Slight fragrance. Growth vigorous and compact. 2 ft.

Paul's Lemon Pillar. (385) CLG.H.T. PAUL 1915. Frau Karl Druschki × Maréchal Niel.
Blooms pale lemon yellow paling to white, very large, full and shapely. Fragrant. Summer flowering. Growth moderately vigorous making an excellent pillar rose. 8 ft.

Paul's Scarlet Climber. (411) PAUL 1916.
Medium sized semi-double flowers; vivid scarlet shaded bright crimson. Slight fragrance. Classified as a rambler though in habit it more resembles a climber. Moderately vigorous to a height of approximately 10 ft. Long period of flowering during Summer. Not remontant.

Peace. (184) H.T. MEILLAND 1945. (George Dickson × Souv. de Claudius Pernet) × (Joanna Hill × Charles P. Kilham) × Margaret McGredy.
Very large double blooms, high centred, cupped in shape when open; golden yellow edges rose-pink. Slight fragrance. An outstanding rose which with light pruning will make a large bush. 5-6 ft. Syn. Gioia; Syn. Gloria Dei; Syn. Mme. A. Meilland.

Peach Glow. (182) FLORI. JACKSON & PERKINS 1960. Goldilocks × Fashion.
Blooms warm peach, cupped, full, 3½ in. across when open, produced in clusters. Slight fragrance. Foliage leathery green. Growth upright and compact. 2 ft. 6 in.

Penelope. (369) SHRUB. PEMBERTON 1924. Ophelia × William Allen Richardson.

Blooms of medium size, semi-double, produced in large clusters. Shell pink fading to white with lemon at centre. Fragrant. Recurrent bloom. Makes a specimen bush up to 6 ft. or is excellent for hedging purposes.

Pepe. (152) H.T. DE RUITER 1961. Amor × Sutter's Gold.
Blooms large and shapely, full with frilled petals. 4 in. across when open. Flame, gold reverse and at base of petals. Fragrant. Glossy dark green foliage. Growth strong and upright. 2 ft. 6 in. to 3 ft.

Perfecta. (16) H.T. KORDES 1957. Spek's Yellow × Karl Herbst.
Large double flowers with high centre; light pink, cream tipped and flushed crimson. Early blooms somewhat indifferent in colour but better later and good in Autumn. Fragrant. Dark glossy leathery foliage. Growth erect and tall 2 ft. 6 in. to 3 ft. Syn. Kordes Perfecta.

Peter Pan (421) See Presumida.

Perle de Montserrat. (419) MIN. DOT 1945. Cecile Brunner × E. rouletti.
Flowers semi-double, open, light pink edged pearl. Dwarf growth up to 12 in.

Phyllis Gold. (103) H.T. H. ROBINSON 1935. Lady Florence Stronge × Julien Potin.
High centred globular full blooms; buttercup yellow shading to cream at edges. Slight fragrance. Rich olive green foliage. Branching habit, growth sturdy up to 2 ft. 6 in.

Piccadilly. (119) H.T. MCGREDY 1959. McGredy's Yellow × Karl Herbst.
Large double blooms of 18-20 petals with high centre; bright red with yellow reverse. Slight fragrance. Dark

handsome green foliage. Growth vigorous and upright. 2 ft. 6 in.

Picture. (105) H.T. MCGREDY 1932. High centred, shapely, full blooms with 30-35 reflexed petals; clear rose pink. No fragrance. Dark glossy foliage. A robust dwarf grower up to 2 ft. Very free from disease.

Pigalle. (311) H.T. MEILLAND 1951. Fantastique × Boudoir. Large full blooms, 4 in. across when open. Magenta edged crimson. Slight fragrance. Foliage bronzy. Growth vigorous. 2 ft. 6 in.

Pink Favourite. (29) H.T. VON ABRAMS 1956. Juno × (George Arends × New Dawn). Large full shapely blooms of 25 petals. Rose pink. Slight fragrance. Very glossy bright green foliage. A sturdy trouble free variety which attains a height of approximately 2 ft. 6 in.

Pinkie. (321) FLORI. SWIM 1947. Blooms medium size, semi-double 15 petals and cupped. Rose pink. Slightly fragrant. Growth dwarf and bushy. 2 ft.

Pink Parfait. (326) FLORI. Hybrid tea type. ARMSTRONG 1960. First Love × Pinocchio. Full petalled medium sized blooms, well formed and with high centres. Pale flushed deeper on margent light apricot reverse. Slight fragrance. Growth compact with abundant mid-green foliage. 2 ft.

Pink Peace. (241) H.T. MEILLAND 1959. (Peace × Monique) × (Peace × Mrs. John Laing). Large full, loose blooms of 50-60 petals. Deep dusty pink. Very fragrant. Leathery foliage. Growth vigorous. 2 ft. 6 in.

Polka. (179) FLORI. MEILLAND 1960. Moulin Rouge × Fashion. Blooms medium size, double with high centre. Claret rose, slight fragrance. Foliage dark green. Growth vigorous and bushy. 2 ft. 6 in.

Polly. (277) H.T. BECKWITH 1927. Ophelia × seedling × Mme. Colette Martinet. Pale yellow long pointed bud developing into large double flower with high centre; cream in colour with pink or light orange centre, fades to white with age. Very fragrant. Growth upright and vigorous. 2 ft. 6 in. to 3 ft.

Poulsen's Bedder. (126) FLORI. S. POULSEN 1948. Orleans Rose × Talisman. Large semi-double blooms; rose-pink in colour. Slight fragrance. Bronzy foliage. Vigorous and compact. 2 ft.

Poulsen's Pink. (115) FLORI. S. POULSEN 1939. Golden Salmon × a yellow Hybrid Tea. Semi-double, cupped shape blooms; pinkish rose with yellow base. Slight fragrance. Light green glossy foliage. Vigorous. 3 ft.

Poulsen's Supreme. (266) FLORI. S. POULSEN 1949. Poulsen's Pink × seedling. Blooms semi-double 3 in. across when open produced in clusters. Pink. Slight fragrance. Foliage light green. Growth vigorous. 2 ft.—2 ft. 6 in.

Première Bal. (141) H.T. MEILLAND 1955. (Fantastique × Caprice) × Peace. Full shapely blooms of 45 petals; ivory with edges, shaded cyclamen rose. Very fragrant. Vigorous and bushy. 2 ft. 6 in.

President Herbert Hoover. (19) H.T. CODDINGTON 1930. Sensation × Souv.

de Claudius Pernet.
Large full shapely blooms of 25 petals. Orange rose and gold with lighter reverse. Good fragrance. Leathery foliage. Growth tall and upright. Inclined to lankiness. 3 ft. An excellent variety for cutting.

Prestige. (125) SHRUB. KORDES 1957.
Rudolph Timm × Brilliant.
Large flat semi-double blooms. Light crimson. Dense dark foliage. Recurrent bloom. A moderate shrub. 3 ft.

Presumida. (421) MIN. DOT 1948.
Eduardo Toda × Pompon de Paris. Small double blooms, mustard yellow to white, centre deep yellow. Dwarf up to 12 in. Syn. Peter Pan.

Prima Ballerina. (46) H.T. TANTAU 1958.
Medium sized double flowers of 20 petals. Cherry pink in colour. Very fragrant. Light green foliage. Growth upright. 3 ft.

Profusion. (129) H.T. MEILLAND 1944.
Mme. Henri Guillot × Signora.
Blooms double, orange-salmon and carmine. Slight fragrance. Glossy foliage. Moderately vigorous. 2 ft. 6 in.

Prosperity. (367) SHRUB. PEMBERTON 1919. Marie Jeanne × Perle des Jardins.
Rosette shaped blooms full and large, produced in clusters. Creamy white. Very fragrant. Growth vigorous and bushy. 5 ft.

Queen Elizabeth. (130) FLORI. Hybrid tea type. LAMMERTS 1954. Charlotte Armstrong × Floradora.
Large full flowers of 40 petals, high centred opening cupped. Carmine rose in bud opening light pink. Produced singly and in clusters. Slight fragrance.

Dark glossy large leathery foliage. Growth very upright. 6 ft.
Suitable for hedging or border. Too tall for formal bed.

Radar. (12) H.T. MEILLAND 1953.
Charles Mallerin × Independence.
Well formed flowers, large and full of 45 petals. Light geranium red flushed scarlet in colour. Fragrant. Vigorous. 2 ft.

Radway Sunrise. (168) SHRUB. WATERHOUSE 1962. Masquerade × unknown seedling.
Blooms large, flat and single, produced freely in large trusses. Recurrent bloom. Yellow at base shading through orange to cherry red. Slight fragrance. Foliage dark and glossy. Growth vigorous and bushy. 4-5 ft.

Raymond Chenault. (380) SEMI-CLIMBER or SHRUB. KORDES 1962. R. kordesii × Montezuma.
Glowing scarlet. Blooms shapely of 17 petals, 4 in. across when open, produced in large clusters. Free flowering and fragrant. Dark green shiny foliage. Vigorous up to 8 ft. Useful as a pillar rose or can be grown as a shrub.

Red Dandy. (128) FLORI. Hybrid tea type. NORMAN 1960.
Medium sized well formed full flowers of 38 petals. Velvety rose red with lighter reverse. Produced in small clusters. Slight fragrance. Medium green foliage. A strong vigorous and attractive variety which appears resistant to disease. 3 ft.

Red Ensign. (3) H.T. NORMAN 1947.
Crimson Glory × Southport.
Large full high centred blooms; dark crimson in colour. Strong damask fragrance. Dark foliage. Inclined to 'ball' when wet, nevertheless capable

of producing blooms of exceptional quality. One of the strongest scented roses in commerce. Growth upright and leggy. 3 ft.

Red Favourite. (113) FLORI. TANTAU 1951. Karl Weinhausen × Cinnabar.
Medium sized semi-double flowers of 12 to 14 petals. Velvety ox-blood red. Slight fragrance. Dark leathery glossy foliage Bushy growth. 2 ft. Syn. foliage Bushy growth. 2 ft. Syn. Hol. landerin; Syn. Schweizer Gruss.

Red Wonder. (114) FLORI. DE RUITER 1955. Better Times × a floribunda seedling.
Large full open flowers, cupped in shape, produced in large clusters. Crimson carmine. Fragrant. Glossy leathery foliage. Vigorous and bushy. 2 ft. 6 ins.

Reina Elisenda (210) See Independence.

Rendez-vous. (72) H.T. MEILLAND 1955. Peace × Europa.
Large full high centred blooms of 50-60 petals. Pink with lighter edge. Fragrant. Rich green leathery foliage. Growth bushy and upright. 2 ft. 6 in. Syn. Day of Triumph.

Rimosa. (131) FLORI. MEILLAND 1959. Goldilocks × Perle de Montserrat.
Semi-double flat blooms of 15-20 petals produced in clusters. Bright yellow fading to cream. Growth robust and bushy. 2 ft.

Rodeo. (58) FLORI. KORDES 1960. Obergartner Wiebicke × Spartan.
Medium sized full blooms. Bright red in colour. Slight fragrance. Light green foliage. Growth compact and bushy. 2 ft.

Rose Gaujard. (127) H.T. GAUJARD 1958. Peace × Opera seedling.
Large full well shaped blooms. White flushed pale pink edged and veined with carmine, silvery reverse. Fragrant. Deep green glossy foliage. Growth very vigorous upright and bushy. 3 ft.

Rosemary Gandy. (132) FLORI. GAUJARD 1958.
Medium sized semi-double flat blooms produced in large clusters. Lemon yellow suffused pale nasturtium red towards the edge. Fragrant. Growth vigorous and upright. 2 ft. 6 in.

Rosemary Rose. (312) FLORI. DE RUITER 1954. Grüss an Teplitz × a floribunda seedling.
Medium sized full flat camellia shaped blooms. Currant red suffused pink. Fragrant. Coppery foliage. An attractive variety, but very subject to mildew. Vigorous. 2 ft. 6 in.

Rouge Meilland (120) See Happiness

Royal Highness. (25 H.T. SWIM & WEEKS 1962. Virgo × Peace.
Blooms large, full and shapely—clear light pink. Fragrant. Growth vigorous. 2½ ft. to 3 ft.

Rubaiyat. (288) H.T. MCGREDY 1946. (McGredy's Scarlet × Mrs. Sam McGredy) × (seedling × Sir Basil McFarland).
Large full long flowers high centre of 25 petals. Rose red with lighter reverse. Very fragrant. Dark leathery foliage. Vigorous and upright. 2 ft. 6 in.

Rugosa Hansa. (348) SHRUB. SCHAUM & VAN TOL 1905.
Blooms full, crimson purple. Very fragrant, produced on short weak stems. Recurrent bloom. Bushy up to 5 ft.

Rumba. (32) FLORI. POULSEN 1959. (Poulsen's Bedder × Floradora) × Masquerade.
Lemon yellow in centre with edges of petals red deepening with age. Blooms 2 in. across many small petals. Fragrant. Uniform growth. 2 ft.

Ruth Leuwerik. (239) FLORI. DE RUITER 1960. Kathe Duvigneau × Rosemary Rose.
Blooms Turkey red, 3 in. across when open, 24 petals, produced in clusters. Fragrant. Foliage bronzy green. Growth bushy and vigorous. 2 ft. 6 in.

Sabrina. 339) H.T. MEILLAND 1960. Bi-colour crimson inside petals, reverse orange and carmine. Blooms globular, full petalled, freely produced. Very fragrant. Foliage dark green. Growth vigorous. 2 ft. 6 in.

Salmon Marvel. (222) FLORI. DE RUITER 1958. Red Pinocchio × Signal Red.
Blooms 2½-3 in. across, full and produced in small clusters. Orange salmon. Growth bushy and vigorous. 2 ft. 6 in.

Salmon Perfection. (34) FLORI. DE RUITER 1950.
Medium sized flat blooms of 25 petals. Scarlet red suffused orange. Dark leathery foliage. Vigorous. 2 ft. 6 in.

Salute. (237) FLORI. MCGREDY 1958. Masquerade × Lady Sylvia.
Blooms small, semi-double produced in large trusses. Cherry and ochre bicolour. Foliage dark green and leathery. Growth vigorous. 3 ft.

Sarabande. (155) FLORI. MEILLAND 1957. Cocorico × Moulin Rouge.
Medium sized semi-double blooms. Very freely produced. Bright orange red. Slight fragrance. Semi-glossy

foliage. A first class bedding variety of dwarf uniform habit of approx. 2 ft.

Sarah Arnot. (322) H.T. CROLL 1957. Ena Harkness × Peace.
Large and full 25 petals. Warm rose pink in colour. Fragrant. Leathery foliage. Vigorous and upright. 2 ft to 2 ft 6 in.

Sarah van Vleet. (357) SHRUB. VAN FLEET 1926. R. rugosa × May Maryland.
Blooms rose pink, large, semi-double, cupped and very fragrant. Recurrent bloom. Growth compact and bushy 6-8 ft.

Scarlet Marvel. (137) FLORI. DE RUITER 1958. Alain × a floribunda seedling.
Medium sized blooms of 45 petals opening flat and produced in clusters. Orange scarlet. Excellent for forcing. Leathery foliage. Vigorous and bushy. 2 ft.

Schlosser's Brilliant (86) See Brilliant.

Schneewittchen (42) See Iceberg.

Schneezwerg. (347) SHRUB. LAMBERT 1912. R. rugosa × E. Snow Dwarf.
Blooms pure white with yellow stamens, semi-double opening flat, produced in clusters. Repeat flowering until scarlet fruits appear in the Autumn. Vigorous compact growth up to 3 ft. Syn. Snow. Dwarf.

Schweizer Gruss (113) See Red Favourite.

Serenade. (289) H.T. BOERNER 1949. Sonata × R.M.S. Queen Mary.
Dark orange buds developing into large cupped shape blooms of 25-30 petals. Coral orange in colour. Slight

fragrance. Glossy leathery foliage. Vigorous and upright. 2 ft. 6 in.

Shepherd's Delight. (217) FLORI. DICKSON 1957. Masquerade seedling × Joanna Hill.
Large semi-double blooms of 15 petals produced in clusters. Flame and yellow. Slight fragrance. Dark green foliage. Vigorous and upright growth. 3 ft.

Sherry. (154) FLORI. MCGREDY 1960. Independence × Orange Sweetheart.
Blooms semi-double, 3 in. across when open produced in trusses. Colour sherry red, dull. Slight fragrance. Growth vigorous and bushy. 2 ft. 6 in. to 3 ft.

Shot Silk. (151) H.T. DICKSON 1924. Hugh Dickson seedling × Sunstar.
Double high centred blooms; cherry cerise with golden yellow base. Very fragrant. Glossy light green foliage. Vigorous and bushy. 2 ft. 6 in.

Silver Lining. (77) H.T. DICKSON 1959. Karl Herbst × Eden Rose seedling.
Large full shapely blooms of 30 petals. Silvery rose in colour with silver reverse. Good fragrance. Vigorous erect growth. 2 ft. 6 in.

Sir Winston Churchill. (176) H.T. DICKSON 1955. Unnamed seedling × Souv. de Denier van der Gon.
Large full blooms with high centre; salmon-pink flushed orange. Fragrant. Dark glossy foliage. Moderately vigorous. 2 ft. 6 in.

Snow Dwarf (347) Schneezwerg

Soldier Boy. (412) SEMI-CLIMBER. LE GRICE 1953. Unnamed seedling × Guinee.
Large single scarlet blooms produced in profusion in early Summer, and then intermittently with fair Autumn display. Rich glossy green foliage. Vigorous 10 ft. An excellent pillar rose.

Soleil. (295) FLORI. MALLERIN 1961.
Blooms semi-double produced in clusters, 4 in. across when open, cinnabar red. Slight fragrance. Foliage light green. Growth vigorous and bushy. 2 ft. 6 in.

Sombrero. (334) FLORI. MCGREDY 1962. Masquerade × Rubaiyat.
Blooms of miniature hybrid tea shape produced in trusses. Full petalled, open 3½ in. across. Cream heavily overlaid rose red. Light green foliage. Vigorous. 2 ft. 6 in.

Soraya. (318) H.T. MEILLAND 1955. (Peace × Floradora) × Grand'mère Jenny.
Large full flowers of 30 petals, cupped in shape; orange red with crimson-red reverse. Slight fragrance. Glossy foliage. Growth bushy and vigorous. 2 ft. to 2 ft. 6 in.

Spanish Beauty (405) See Mme. Gregoire Staechelin.

Spartan. (136) FLORI. BOERNER 1955. Geranium Red × Fashion.
Large blooms of 30 petals, shapely in bud produced singly and in clusters; orange-red shaded coral. Very fragrant. Glossy dark leathery foliage. Vigorous and tall up to 4 ft.

Spectacular (395) See Danse du Feu.

Spek's Yellow. (218) H.T. VERSCHUREN-PECHTOLD 1950. Golden Rapture × unnamed seedling.
Small to medium sized full shapely blooms of 35 petals. Deep yellow in colour. Fragrant. Glossy leathery foliage. An excellent rose for cutting

and one which keeps its colour well. Growth tall and leggy. 3 ft. Syn. Golden Sceptre.

Spinosissima - Double Yellow. (346 and 352) SHRUB.

Blooms small, double; yellow with green carpels in centre. Strong scent. Makes a small bush up to 3 ft.

Spinosissima Lutea Maxima. (353) SHRUB.

Deep yellow blooms 2 in. across, single. Rich green foliage. Will make an excellent shrub up to 4 to 5 ft.

Stadt Rosenheim. (39) H.T. KORDES 1961. Korona × Spartan.

Blooms medium size, full petalled and shapely. Orange red. Slight fragrance. Foliage large, dark green. Growth vigorous 2 ft. 6 in.

Starfire. (97) FLORI. hybrid tea type. LAMMERTS 1958. Charlotte Armstrong × unnamed seedling.

Blooms large, urn-shaped, 25-30 petals produced singly and in clusters. Currant red. Fragrant. Glossy foliage. Vigorous and tall. 3 ft.

Stella. (287) H.T. TANTAU 1959. Seedling × seedling.

Large full blooms of 36 petals, with high centre, well shaped; cream flushed pink with carmine edges to petals. Slight fragrance. Plentiful dark green foliage. Growth vigorous and upright. 2 ft. 6 in. to 3 ft.

Sterling Silver. (331) H.T. FISHER 1957. Seedling × Peace.

Blooms shapely, full and medium size; lilac. Very fragrant. Moderately vigorous. 2 ft. Best grown under glass.

St. Pauli. (362) FLORI. KORDES 1959. Masquerade × Karl Herbst.

Small semi-double blooms; carmine in colour splashed light yellow. Slight fragrance. Large leathery medium green foliage. Vigorous and upright. 3 ft.

Summer Song. (230) FLORI. DICKSON 1962.

Blooms semi-double, large 4 in. across when open, produced in trusses. Orange and pale gold. Slight fragrance. Growth vigorous. 2 ft. 6 in. to 3 ft.

Summer Sunshine. (47) H.T. SWIM 1961. (Buccaneer × Lemon Chiffon.

Blooms large, high centred and full. Deep yellow. Slight fragrance. Medium green foliage. Vigorous and upright. 3 ft.

Sundance. (302) FLORI. S. POULSEN 1954. Poulsen's Supreme × Eugene Furst.

Medium sized double blooms of 22 petals, produced in clusters; orange-yellow changing to bright rose pink with age. Slight fragrance. Light green foliage. Vigorous and upright. 3 ft.

Super Star. (290) H.T. TANTAU 1960.

Well formed medium sized full blooms of 33 petals; pure light vermilion in colour. Sweet fragrance. Glossy dark green foliage, most attractive. Blooms freely produced on long stems single and in clusters. Growth vigorous and tall. 4 ft. Syn. Tropicana.

Suspense. (185) H.T. MEILLAND 1960.

Very large deep scarlet blooms with yellow reverse, full and shapely. Growth robust and branching. 2 ft. 6 in.

Sutters Gold. (292) H.T. SWIM 1950. Charlotte Armstrong × Signora.

Bud orange red, developing to golden yellow flower, shapely, full, large and long. Very fragrant. Foliage leathery and dark green. Growth moderately vigorous and tall. 3ft. making slender tree.

Suzon Lotthe. (328) H.T. MEILLAND 1951. Peace × (Signora × Mrs. John Laing).
Blooms large and globular, 60 petals, pearl pink flushed deeper pink towards edges of petals. Very fragrant. Foliage dark green. Moderately vigorous. 2 ft.

Sweet Repose. (219) FLORI. DE RUITER 1955. Golden Rapture × unnamed floribunda seedling.
Medium sized full blooms, cupped in shape, produced in large cluster, of 27 petals. Maize yellow tinted carmine changing completely to carmine with age. Sweet fragrance. Leathery foliage. Growth vigorous. 2 ft. 6 in. to 3 ft. Syn. The Optimist.

Sweet Sultan. (386) CL. H.T. EACOTT 1958. Independence × Honour Bright.
Blooms single, 4 in. across, produced in large clusters. Crimson shaded maroon. Recurrent bloom. Very fragrant. A moderately vigorous pillar rose up to 8 ft.

Symphonie. (190) H.T. MEILLAND 1951. Peace × (Signora × Mrs. John Laing).
Large full, globular blooms of 25 petals. Pink veined carmine-pink. Very fragrant. Glossy leathery foliage. Growth moderately vigorous. 2 ft.

Taffeta. (38) H.T. LAMMERTS 1947. Mrs. Sam McGredy × President Herbert Hoover. Semi-double blooms of 16--22 petals of medium size. Colour variable from pink to yellow. Fragrant Leathery bronzy green foliage. Vigorous upright. 2 ft. 6 in.

Tally Ho. (286) H.T. SWIM 1948. Charlotte Armstrong × unnamed seedling.
Large full blooms with high centre, of 35 petals. Rose red with cardinal red reverse. Strong fragrance. Leathery foliage. Very vigorous and upright. 3 ft to 4 ft.

Tambourine. (144) FLORI. A DICKSON 1959. Independence seedling × Karl Herbst.
Large semi-double blooms of 18 petal produced in trusses. Cherry-red and yellow. Slight fragrance. Dark foliage. Vigorous. 2 ft. 6 in.

Tapestry. (27) H.T. FISHER 1958. Peace × Mission Bells.
Blooms cupped, large and full, 35-40 petals. Colour a combination of red, yellow and pink. Fragrant. Foliage glossy. Growth vigorous and bushy. 2 ft.

Teenager. (313) H.T. ARNOT 1958. Ena Harkness × Sutter's Gold.
Medium sized full blooms of 25 petals; rose pink, yellow at base, reverse cream. Very fragrant. Deep green leathery foliage. Growth vigorous and branching. 2 ft. to 2 ft. 6 in.

Texas Centennial. (79) H.T. A. F. WATKINS 1935. President Herbert Hoover sport.
Well formed full flowers of 25 petals; vermilion red with lighter centre with some gold shading. Fragrant. Vigorous and upright. 2 ft. 6 in.

Thais (251) H.T. MEILLAND 1954. Mme. Kriloff × (Peace × Geneve).
Reddish apricot in bud developing into full large cupped shaped blooms; buff yellow suffused strawberry pink. Fragrant. Dark leathery foliage. Moderately vigorous. 2 ft. to 2 ft. 6 in. Syn. Lady Elgin.

The Doctor. (139) H.T. HOWARD & SMITH 1936. Mrs. J.D. Eiselle × Los Angeles.
Large well formed blooms 30 petals, pink and very fragrant. Moderately vigorous and free flowering.

The Mouse (33) See Grey Pearl.

The New Dawn. (383) CLIMBER. SPORT of DR. VAN FLEET.
Ovoid blooms shapely, but small, full petalled, produced in clusters. Blush pink. Fragrant. Foliage small dark green and glossy. An excellent pillar rose or semi-climber. 10 ft. Repeat flowering.

The Optimist (219) See Sweet Repose.

The People. (160) FLORI. H.T. type. TANTAU 1954. Tantau's Triumph × (Kathe Duvigneau × Tantau's Triumph).
Blooms large 3 in., full (26 petals), produced singly and in small trusses. Crimson shaded deep pink. Slight fragrance. Foliage light green. Growth bushy and vigorous. 2 ft. 6 in.

Tiffany. (142) H.T. LINDQUIST 1954. Charlotte Armstrong × Girona.
Large full shapely blooms with high centre, 25-30 petals; deep pink with lighter shadings. Very fragrant. Dark foliage. Growth vigorous and upright. 3 ft.

Tivoli. (310) FLORI. S. POULSEN 1955. Poulsen's Supreme × (Souv. De Claudius Denoyel × Hvissinge-Rose).
Medium sized well formed full blooms of 24 petals, produced in clusters; warm rose-pink with yellow centre. Fragrant. Dark glossy foliage. Very vigorous. 3 ft. 6 in.

Tony Lander. (162) FLORI. POULSEN 1959. Independence × Circus.
Blooms full petalled, 3½ in. across when open, produced in clusters. Rich salmon edged scarlet. Slight fragrance. Growth vigorous and uniform. 2 ft. 6 in.

Traumland (95) See Dreamland.

Tropicana (290) See Super Star.

Tzigane. (186) H.T. MEILLAND 1956. Peace × J.B. Meilland.
Large full globular blooms; rose-red with yellow reverse. Fragrant. Dark glossy leathery foliage. Moderately vigorous and bushy. 2 ft.

United Nations. (232) FLORI. LEENDERS 1949. Nathalie Nypels × Rosamunde.
Medium sized full open blooms, produced in large trusses. Salmon-pink flushed cream. Fragrant. Glossy foliage, somewhat susceptible to mildew. Vigorous and upright. 3 ft.

Vanity. (377) SHRUB. PEMBERTON 1920. Chateau de Glos Vougeot × seedling.
Blooms almost single, flat and 3 in. across. Rose pink. Continuous flowering. Very fragrant. A vigorous variety, with strong arching stems up to 8 ft.

Vick's Caprice. (364) H.P. VIC 1891. Blooms lilac rose striped white and carmine. Large, full and cupped. Fragrant. Intermittent bloom. Moderate growth for a hybrid perpetual up to 2 ft. 6 in.

Vilia. (212) FLORI. H. ROBINSON 1958. Medium sized single blooms produced in small clusters. Pale scarlet with slight yellow at base of petals. Fragrant. Growth moderate and bushy. 2 ft.

Virgo. (213) H.T. MALLERIN 1947.
Blanche Mallerin × Neige Parfum.
Shapely long blooms of 30 petals,
produced on long stems excellent for
cutting. White, occasionally flushed
very pale pink. Slight fragrance. Dark
leathery foliage. Growth moderate. 2
ft.

Vive la France. (264) H.T. MALLERIN
1944. Shining Star × Mme. Arthaud.
Blooms large and double; bi-colour
purplish red with yellow reverse.
Glossy foliage. 2 ft 6 in.

Vogue. (233) FLORI. BOERNER 1951.
Pinocchio × Crimson Glory.
Medium sized shapely blooms of 25
petals, produced in clusters. Cherry
coral in colour. Fragrant. Glossy foliage. Growth vigorous and upright. 2 ft.
6 in.

War Dance. (26) H.T. SWIM & WEEKS
1961. Roundelay × Crimson Glory.
Blooms of orange scarlet, medium size,
full. Slight fragrance. Normal green
foliage. Growth robust and spreading.
2 ft. 6 in.

Wendy Cussons. (223) H.T. GREGORY
1959.
Blooms long pointed and shapely 3½
in. 37 petals. Freely produced. Cerise.
Very fragrant. Dark green glossy
foliage. Growth vigorous and branching. 2 ft. 6 in. to 3 ft.

Westminster. (143) H.T. ROBINSON
1959. Gay Crusader × Peace.
Large full globular blooms; bi-colour
cherry red with paler reverse. Splashed
yellow. Very fragrant. Growth branching. 2 ft. 6 in.

White Knight, (240) See Message.

Woburn Abbey. (169) FLORI. SIDEY
1961. Masquerade × Fashion.
Blooms 3 in. across, cupped, 23
small petals. Coppery orange shaded
gold. Moderate fragrance. Habit bushy
with small dark green foliage. Vigorous. 2 ft. 6 in.

Yellowhammer. (122) FLORI. MCGRE-
DY 1956. Poulsen's Yellow × unnamed
seedling.
Well formed blooms, medium sized,
semi-double produced in clusters;
Moderately vigorous. 2 ft.

Yvonne Rabier. (234) FLORI. TURBAT
1910. R. wichuraiana × a polyantha.
Loose flat blooms of medium size,
semi-double produced in trusses. Pure
white slightly tinted sulphur yellow at
base. Fragrant. Rich green slender
foliage, practically evergreen. Vigorous and bushy. Will make specimen
bush up to 3 ft.

Zambra. (156) FLORI. MEILLAND 1961.
Blooms flat, semi-double, of medium
size produced in trusses. Orange
bright yellow reverse – a striking colour. Slight fragrance. Vigorous and
bushy. 2 ft. 6 in.

Zephirine Drouhin. (394) BOURBON.
BIZOT 1868.
Medium sized flat blooms, semi-double.
Bright Carmine pink. Fragrant. Soft
light foliage. Thornless. Vigorous.
10-12 ft. Suitable for wall or trellis.

Zigeuner Knabe. (365) SHRUB. LAM-
BERT 1909. (Gypsy Boy)
Blooms dark violet purple. Medium
sized and full petalled. Summer flowering. Growth vigorous and bushy. 5
ft Syn. Gipsy Boy.

Zwergkönig (418) See Dwarf King.

BASIC COLOURS

To facilitate tracing roses, of which only the colour is known, the following grouping according to basic colours will be found helpful.

WHITE AND WHITE FLUSHED PINK OR CREAM

Hybrid Teas
Ardelle
Coy Colleen
Frau Karl Druschki
Garden Party
McGredy's Ivory
Memoriam

Message
Polly
Virgo

Floribunda
Iceberg
Ivory Fashion
Yvonne Rabier

Shrubs
Blanc Double de
 Coubert
Frühlingsanfang
Prosperity
Schneezwerg

CREAM TO YELLOW

Hybrid Teas
Belle Blonde
Buccaneer
Burnaby
Dorothy Peach
Dr. A. J. Verhage
Dries Verschuren
Ellinor Le Grice
Ethel Sanday
Fantasia
Fred Howard
Fred Streeter
Gertrude Gregory
Gold Crown
Golden Dawn
Golden Giant
Golden Masterpiece
Golden Melody
Grand'mere Jenny
Isobel Harkness
King's Ransom
Lydia
McGredy's Yellow
Moonbeam
Peace

Phyllis Gold
Spek's Yellow
Summer Sunshine
Sutter's Gold

Floribundas
Allgold
Angela
Chanelle
Dairy Maid
Faust
Gold Cup
Gold Marie
Golden Jewel
Goldilocks
Honeymoon
June Bride
Rimosa
Sundance
Sweet Repose
Yellowhammer

Shrubs
Chinatown
Erfurt

Foetida
Frühlingsduft
Frühlingsgold
Nevada
Ormiston Roy
Spinosissima
 Double Yellow
Spinosissima
 Lutea Maxima

Climbers & Ramblers
Alberic Barbier
Elegance
Emily Gray
Golden Showers
High Noon
Leverkusen
Maigold
Mermaid
Paul's Lemon Pillar

Miniatures
Baby Gold Star
Presumida

APRICOT, BUFF AND ORANGE SHADES

Hybrid Teas
Andre le Troquer
Bayadere
Bettina
Chantre
Cynthia Brooke
Diamond Jubilee
Doreen
Fanny Blankers Koen
Gordon Eddie
Hawaii
Helen Traubel
Lady Belper
Marjorie Le Grice
Mme. Henri Guillot
Mojave

Mrs. Sam McGredy
My Lady
Party Dress
Thais

Floribundas
Alison Wheatcroft
Circus
Copper Delight
Countess of Dalkeith
Fantan
Orangeade
Orange Sensation
Peach Glow
Rosemary Gandy
Summer Song

Woburn Abbey
Zambra

Shrubs
Buff Beauty
Friedrich Heyer
Grandmaster

Climbers
Gloire de Dijon
Meg
Mme Edouard Herriot

Miniatures
Colibri

LIGHT PINK

Hybrid Teas
Anne Letts
Columbus Queen
Confidence
Dorothy Anderson
Emily
First Love
Grace de Monaco
Lunelle
Margaret
Ophelia
Premier Bal
Rendezvous

Royal Highness
Silver Lining
Stella
Suzon Lotthe
Taffeta

Floribundas
Bonny Maid
Ma Perkins

Shrubs
Gay Vista
Penelope

Climbers and Ramblers
Albertine
Blossom Time
Clair Matin
Conrad F. Meyer
Dr. W. Van Fleet
Mme. Gregoire
   Staechelin
The New Dawn

Miniatures
Perle de Montserrat

SALMON, SALMON PINK TO VERMILION

Hybrid Teas
Aztec
Comtesse Vandal
Elysium
Fritz Thiedemann
Garvey
Gentle
Invitation
Lal
Michele Meilland

Mischief
Montezuma
Serenade
Sir Winston Churchill
Super Star

Floribundas
Anna Wheatcroft
Ascot
Border Coral

Dany Robin
Display
Dreamland
Farandole
Fashion
Hansestadt Bremen
Happy Anniversary
Miracle
Salmon Marvel
Salmon Perfection

Spartan
Toni Lander
United Nations

Climbers
Lady Waterlow

Poly. Poms.
Cameo
Gloria Mundi

Shrubs
Kathleen Ferrier
Nymphenberg

DEEP PINK

Hybrid Teas
Bacchus
Ballet
Dame de Coeur
Dr. Debat
Eden Rose
Gail Borden
Hebe
June Park
Lady Maysie Robinson
Lady Sylvia
La Jolla
Marella
Mme Caroline Testout
Monique
My Choice
Perfecta
Picture
Pink Favourite
Pink Peace

Prima Ballerina
Rubaiyat
Sarah Arnot
Shot Silk
Symphonie
The Doctor
Tiffany

Floribundas
August Seebauer
Cecile Brunner
Celebration
Chic
Dearest
Flamenco
Jiminy Cricket
My Fair Lady
Paddy McGredy
Pinkie
Pink Parfait

Poulsen's Bedder
Poulsen's Supreme
Queen Elizabeth
Tivoli

Shrubs
Buisman's Triumph
Cantab
Elmshorn
Frühlingsmorgen
Sarah Van Fleet
Vanity

Climbers and Ramblers
Aloha
American Pillar
Köln am Rhein
Lady Gay
Zephirine Drouhin

CARMINE AND RED

Hybrid Teas
Betty Uprichard
Charlotte Armstrong
Claude
Duet
Gay Lady
Jolie Madame
Lucy Cramphorn

Magali
Paris-Match

Floribundas
Jane Lazenby
Profusion
Sherry
Vogue

Shrubs
Parfum de l'Hay

Climbers
Danse des Sylphes

Miniatures
Dwarf King

SHADES OF SCARLET RED

Hybrid Teas
Baccara
Bingo

Brilliant
Champs Elysees
Christian Dior

Christopher Stone
Ena Harkness
Fandango

Garten Zauber
Happiness
High Society
John S. Armstrong
Karl Herbst
Konrad Adenauer
Lady Zia
La Jolie
Milord
New Yorker
Opera
Radar
Red Ensign
Soroya
Suspense
Tally Ho
Texas Centennial
War Dance
Wendy Cussons

Floribundas
Alain
Allotria
Ama
Anne Poulsen
Burning Love
Carrousel
Chanteclerc
Concerto
Diamant
Diablotin

Dickson's Flame
Donald Prior
El Capitan
Embrasement
Evelyn Fison
Fervid
Feurio
Firecracker
Fire King
First Choice
Florence Mary Morse
Frensham
Hassan
Highlight
Independence
Karen Poulsen
Korona
Lili Marlene
Lubeck
Meteor
Miss France
Ohlala
Orange Triumph
Paprika
Polka
Red Dandy
Red Favourite
Red Wonder
Rodeo
Rosemary Gandy
Ruth Leuwerik

Sarabande
Scarlet Marvel
Soleil
Starfire
Stadt Rosenheim
The People
Vilia

Shrubs
Berlin
Cocktail
Dorothy Wheatcroft
Flammentanz
F. J. Grootendorst
Gustav Frahm
Heidelberg
Henry Morse
Kassel
Prestige

Climbers and Ramblers
Allen Chandler
Crimson Conquest
Crimson Shower
Danse du Feu
Dortmund
Excelsa
Hamburger Phoenix
Hugh Dickson
Paul's Scarlet Climber
Raymond Chenault
Soldier Boy

DARK VELVETY RED

Hybrid Teas
Bonne Nuit
Chrysler Imperial
Crimson Glory
Josephine Bruce
Mirandy
Mme. Louis Laperriere

Nocturne
Pigalle

Floribundas
Dusky Maiden
Moulin Rouge

Shrubs
Zigeuner Knabe

Climbers
Guinee
Parkdirektor Riggers
Sweet Sultan

BICOLOURS RED AND YELLOW, AND RED AND SILVER

Hybrid Teas
Autumn

Bajazzo
Charles Gregory

Chicago Peace
Cleopatra

Elsa Arnot
Fascinating
Flaming Sunset
Forty-Niner
Grand Gala
Huntsman
Isabel de Ortiz
Love Song
Mahagona
McGredy's Sunset
Miss Ireland
Mme. L. Dieudonne
Mme. Rene Coty
Pepe
Piccadilly

President Herbert
   Hoover
Rose Gaujard
Sabrina
Tapestry
Teenager
Tzigane
Vive la France
Westminster

Floribundas
Condesa de Sastago
Daily Sketch
Dainty Maid
Enterprise

Fanfare
June Opie
Masquerade
Rumba
St. Pauli
Salute
Shepherd's Delight
Sombrero
Tambourine

Shrub
Radway Sunrise

Miniature
Baby Masquerade

SHADES OF LAVENDER

Hybrid Teas
Grey Pearl
Lilac Time
Sterling Silver

Floribundas
Cyclamen
Lavender Girl
Lavender Pinocchio
Lilac Charm

Shrubs
Lavender Lassie
Magenta
Rubrifolia Carminetta
Rugosa Hansa
Vick's Caprice

INDEX

The first column of numerals gives the page numbers on which the descriptions appear and the second column gives the page numbers on which the illustrations are to be found.